WALKING IN SARDINIA

About the Author

Paddy Dillon is a prolific walker and guidebook writer, with over 50 books to his name and contributions to many more. He also writes regularly for outdoor magazines and has appeared on radio and television.

He uses a palmtop computer to write as he walks. This makes his descriptions, written at the very point at which the reader uses them, highly accurate and easy to follow on the ground.

Paddy is an indefatigable long-distance walker who has walked all of Britain's National Trails and several major European trails. He lives on the fringes of the English Lake District and has led guided walking holidays and has walked throughout Europe, as well as in Nepal, Tibet and the Rocky Mountains of Canada and the US. Paddy is a member of the Outdoor Writers and Photographers Guild.

Other Cicerone guides by the author

WALKING IN SARDINIA

by

Paddy Dillon

2 POLICE SQUARE, MILNTHORPE, CUMBRIA LA7 7PY
www.cicerone.co.uk

© Paddy Dillon 2011
First edition 2011
ISBN: 978 1 85284 619 0

Printed by KHL Printing, Singapore
A catalogue record for this book is available from the British Library.
All photographs are by the author unless otherwise stated.

Advice to Readers

Readers are advised that, while every effort is made by our authors to ensure the accuracy of guidebooks as they go to print, changes can occur during the lifetime of an edition. Please check Updates on this book's page on the Cicerone website (www.cicerone.co.uk) before planning your trip. We would also advise that you check information about such things as transport, accommodation and shops locally. Even rights of way can be altered over time. We are always grateful for information about any discrepancies between a guidebook and the facts on the ground, sent by email to info@cicerone.co.uk or by post to Cicerone, 2 Police Square, Milnthorpe LA7 7PY, United Kingdom.

Warning

Mountain walking can be a dangerous activity carrying a risk of personal injury or death. It should be undertaken only by those with a full understanding of the risks and with the training and experience to evaluate them. While every care and effort has been taken in the preparation of this guide, the user should be aware that conditions can be highly variable and can change quickly, materially affecting the seriousness of a mountain walk. Therefore, except for any liability which cannot be excluded by law, neither Cicerone nor the author accept liability for damage of any nature (including damage to property, personal injury or death) arising directly or indirectly from the information in this book.

To call out the Mountain Rescue in Sardinia, call 118 and ask for *intervento tecnico in montagna*.

Front cover: The rock walls of Punta Cusidore rise above fields between Oliena and Dorgali (Walk 4)

CONTENTS

Map Key

━━━━━━━	major roads
━━━━━━━	walking route
··················	adjoining walk
━ ━ ━ ━ ━	alternative route/extension
─ ─ ─ ─ ─	link
··················	dirt track
─ ─ ─ ─ ─	path
··················	seasonal river
──────	river
⬭	sea
▥▥▥▥▥▥▥	tunnel
⬭	town
▲	peak on (or near) a walk
▪	building
●	landmark feature
●	funtana(spring) pool
→	route direction
→	direction arrow
Ⓢ Ⓕ	start point/finish point
ⓢⓕ	start and finish point
ⒶⓈ	alternative start point
ⒶⒻ	alternative finish point
ⒶⓈⒻ	alternative start and finish point

Contour Key

	800–1000m		1800–2000m
	600–800m		1600–1800m
	400–600m		1400–1600m
	200–400m		1200–1400m
	0–200m		1000–1200m
	sea level		

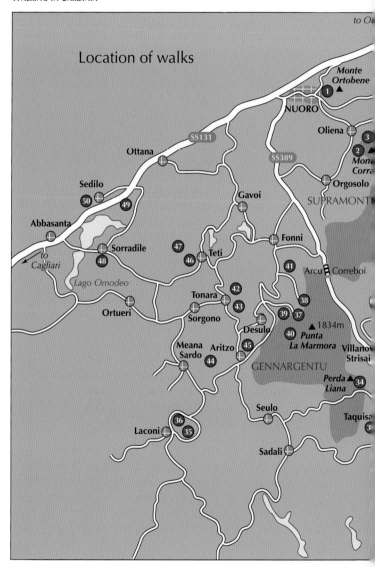

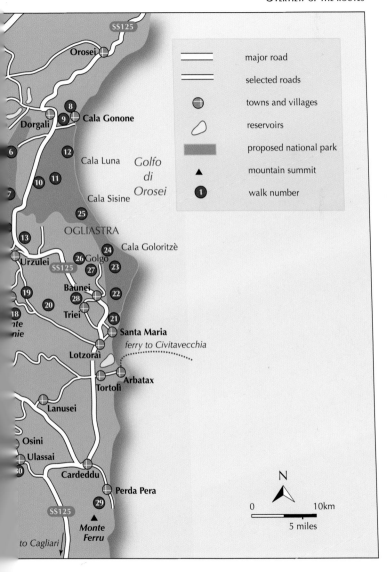

*Looking along the crest from Punta Perdu Abes to
Punta La Marmora (Walk 42)*

INTRODUCTION

Looking south-west from a viewpoint on Monte Ortobene to Monte Corrasi and its neighbours (Walk 1)

Sardinia, lying to the west of Italy, is one of the largest islands in the Mediterranean. Its sun-drenched beaches have long been renowned for their beauty, and for many decades travellers took a rather romantic view of the hard, simple life led by the island's shepherds. Only in recent years have visitors to the island really started trying to penetrate the complex network of narrow, rugged mountain paths that weave through woods and the dense scrub of the *macchia*, discovering ancient hand-carved rock tombs, tumbled nuraghic (megalithic) towers and settlements, and cosy little *pinnettus* used throughout the centuries as simple shepherd's dwellings.

Until recently walkers often experienced great problems trying to follow difficult routes without the benefit of signposts or markers. All agreed that the uplands were wild, remote and often stunningly, savagely beautiful, while at the same time being incredibly difficult to access and frustratingly awkward to explore. Now, however, to walkers' great relief, signposts and waymarked trails have become available in many places, and more and more remote areas are becoming better known.

This guidebook explores the wildest, highest and most remote parts of Sardinia, using a mixture of trodden and un-trodden routes, as well as newly signposted and waymarked trails. The area covered, lying east of the centre of Sardinia, includes the stunning cliff coastline of Ogliastra, the barren Supramonte further inland, and the broad, high mountains of Gennargentu. This region contains some of the best and most popular walks on the island, and was recently proposed as a national park. Good roads from nearby towns, such as Nuoro, allow access to the region, while winding mountain roads penetrate to the most remote parts. Surprisingly, most villages offer a wide range of facilities and often have quite good bus services. This guidebook aims to encourage walkers to visit and explore the villages, use the local services and facilities, and enjoy a wide range of walking routes, to suit all abilities, while exploring the area's rich and varied countryside.

LOCATION

DH Lawrence described Sardinia as being 'lost between Europe and Africa and belonging nowhere'. More precisely, Sardinia lies west of Italy, south of France and Corsica, east of the Balearic Islands and Spain, and north of the African countries of Tunisia and Algeria. The island's location attracted early settlers from three distinct parts of the Mediterranean – the Italian and Iberian peninsulas, and North Africa. Each had their own culture and traditions, and yet the island was large enough to absorb these, and all other invaders and settlers, throughout the centuries.

Sardinia is one of the largest Mediterranean islands, being second only to Sicily in size. Some islands are small enough to be explored comfortably in holidays lasting a week or two, but this simply isn't the case with

Sardinia is renowned for its astounding coastline and rugged landscapes

Sardinia. The island is huge, and the best way for British visitors to appreciate this is to remember that it is about the same size as Wales, but rather more difficult to get around.

Exploring Sardinia in depth would take a lifetime, which is why this guidebook concentrates on the region where the best walking opportunities are within easy reach of each other. In summer, when the heat is ferocious at sea level, the high mountains and cooler air can be gained with relative ease. In winter, when the mountains are covered in snow, the low-lying parts and coastal fringe feature much kinder weather.

The high mountains are often composed of highly contorted schist containing bands of quartz

GEOLOGY

In the area covered by this guidebook, the oldest rocks are complex, contorted, crumbling schist, occurring mainly in the highest mountains of Gennargentu. In some places there are significant granite intrusions, and this rock either forms prominent outcrops or crumbles into coarse sand and gravel. Rising from the sea are massive limestone cliffs, and the same rock extends far inland, rising to high mountains, often incredibly steep, rugged and arid. In some places remnants of this limestone layer sit on top of the crumbling schist and form distinctive *taccu* ('shoe-heel') summits, which

are steep-sided and flat-topped. Some areas, particularly around the Golgo plateau and Dorgali, are covered by relatively recent basalt lava flows.

HISTORY

In common with most Mediterranean islands, Sardinia has a long and complex history. It was visited by palaeolithic hunter-gatherers, who established no permanent settlements.

15

Inside one of the domus de janas *at the Necropoli di Ispiluncas (Walk 50)*

Continuous habitation dates from neolithic times, around 6000BC. Interestingly, these settlers travelled from places as far apart as Italy, Iberia and Africa. They sometimes formed alliances and were sometimes in dispute with each other. The most notable neolithic structures on the island are the square-cut rock tombs known as *domus de janas* ('fairy house') and *tomba dei giganti* ('giants' tomb'). Dwellings, on the other hand, were simple circular huts, with low stone foundations topped by a 'wigwam' of thatched branches, similar to the pinnettus used by shepherds today.

By the Bronze Age, around 1500BC, villages of circular huts were often huddled close together for mutual defence, and stout *nuraghe* (stone towers) were built as central

refuges. Immense boulders were used in their construction. Many remain in good shape, some have been partially restored, while others have tumbled, making them difficult to locate, although around 7000 are known.

Phoenician traders visited Sardinia from 1000BC, establishing coastal settlements at first, but encountering resistance as they moved further inland. When Sardinians attacked their ports after 500BC, the Phoenicians sought help from the Carthaginians. Together they conquered most of the island, except for the highest and most rugged mountain areas, which proved difficult for all subsequent invaders to control. After the First Punic War in 238BC, the Romans took control of Sardinia and it became a Roman province for seven centuries. The highest and most mountainous region was deemed 'barbarian', and this is where the bulk of the routes in this guidebook are located.

With the collapse of Roman authority, Vandals settled in parts of Sardinia from AD456, but were dislodged after AD534, when Sardinia became part of the Byzantine empire. The 'barbarian' region was the last to be brought under control, and the last to be converted to Christianity. As Arabs spread around the Mediterranean, Sardinia organised its own resistance. Coastal raids commenced in AD703, and the population moved inland for safety. By the year 900 Sardinia had split into four distinct regions, referred to as *giudicati*. Each region allied itself with particular powers, including the city states of Genoa and Pisa.

As various European powers jostled for supremacy, Sardinia came under Aragonese influence and found itself part of the Kingdom of Sardinia and Corsica in 1324. Political turmoil throughout the 14th century led to the formation of the kingdom of Arborea, which encompassed the whole of Sardinia, except for the towns of Cagliari and Alghero, with Eleonora d'Arborea as effective ruler. However, Spanish influence and control in Sardinia stretched through to the early 18th century. During the War of Spanish Succession, Austria and Spain wrestled for control before the island passed to the dukes of Savoy, princes

of Piedmont, by 1718. This move led to Sardinia being incorporated into Piedmont, and both areas were jointly referred to as the Kingdom of Sardinia.

A succession of wars led to the unity of states on the Italian peninsula, and by 1861 the Kingdom of Sardinia became the Kingdom of Italy. After the Second World War Italy became a republic in 1946, and Sardinia was granted a greater measure of autonomy than any other region. The coastal areas were malarial until 1950, but the disease was wiped out by a comprehensive spraying program. Tourism developed

Sardinia's history and heritage is often celebrated by murals painted on the walls of houses

from that point, but wavering economics caused many Sardinians to leave the island. In the 1960s new industries flourished, including oil refineries and chemical plants. Some marshland areas were reclaimed for agriculture, while some agricultural areas were covered by industrial estates. On the highest and most rugged parts of the island, there was little change, though rural populations declined as people moved to the expanding urban areas. There are almost 1.7 million people living in Sardinia, mostly in a handful of towns, but there are also ten million visiting tourists each year, most of whom come for the beaches.

LANDSCAPE

Sardinia's landscapes are rich and varied. Most upland regions are well forested, but many parts feature dense, bushy scrub, or macchia, and plenty of bare rock. Most of the routes in this guidebook climb above 500m (1640ft), and may climb above 1000m (3280ft), with three routes converging on the highest mountain, Punta La Marmora, at 1834m (6017ft).

Some of the lower sunny slopes have been adapted to support vineyards, while low-lying areas are often intensively cultivated, producing all types of fruit and vegetables. The forested areas often feature clearings, which might be stocked with goats or pigs. Sheep and cattle are generally grazed in grassier areas.

No matter what types of landscape are encountered, the overall aspect is remote and rugged, removed from habitation. The terrain is ideal for walking, as long as good tracks and paths are followed. Trying to walk across country, without the benefit of trodden routes, often results in great difficulties.

Outside the area covered by this guidebook the mountains are lower, but no less rugged. As fewer walkers head for these other areas, there are not as many waymarked trails – none at all in some places – and fewer opportunities to discover a good range of walking routes. However, there are plenty of beaches that are much easier to reach than most of the beaches visited on routes in this guidebook.

TREES AND FLOWERS

Sardinia's forests are overwhelmingly oak, ranging from evergreen holm oak to thick-barked cork oak, with deciduous oaks favouring the higher mountains. In some places pines are notable, either natural or in plantations. In limestone areas, gnarled juniper trees are common, and their trunks and branches endure long after they die. Lentisc trees often form dense, bushy scrub. Tall, straight alders generally grow alongside mountain watercourses, while at lower levels dense growths of oleasters almost choke the seasonal riverbeds. Cultivated trees include olives and all manner of fruit

Young holm oaks often have spiky leaves as a defence against grazing animals

BIRDS

Sardinia is well placed on migration routes, so that between September and March all kinds of birds can be observed.

There are great differences between the species that are attracted to the coast and to the mountains. Sardinia's low-lying marshlands and lagoons provide a habitat for the greatest number of species, including flamingos and herons, but are not visited on any of the walking routes in this guidebook. The cliff coast is often difficult to access, but provides good nesting sites for a variety of species.

Inland, opportunities to observe birds increases, and wooded areas support woodpigeons, woodpeckers and partridges. Open areas may feature shrikes, finches and warblers, with kites and kestrels hunting. Cliffs are often home to choughs and crag martins. The mountains are the preserve of ravens, while raptors include sparrowhawks, goshawks, eagles and vultures.

and nut trees. Oranges and lemons are grown as much for their ornamental value in gardens as they are in fruit groves. Almond trees sprout masses of flowers in spring.

The low, bushy, impenetrable macchia is often rich in species. These include aromatic and colourful lavender and rosemary, bushy broom and sticky cistus, dense and thorny species, and a range of delicate and colourful flowers that come and go through spring and summer, including crocuses and cyclamen. Some areas may be completely overwhelmed with stout asphodels.

ANIMALS

Sardinia's countryside is extensively grazed by domestic stock, including sheep, goats, cattle, pigs and horses. Some feral goats might be seen, as well as herds of horses grazing high in the mountains, and in one particular region, Sarcidano, an unusual breed, the Sarcidano horse, survives. Very occasionally it might be possible to glimpse wild boar, but these shun human contact. A rare breed of wild

19

Goats graze throughout Sardinia, and their milk is often used to make a variety of cheeses

sheep known as *mouflon* has been reintroduced to Sardinia, along with small red deer, or *cerv*.

There are snakes in Sardinia, more noticeable on the hottest days and absent on colder days. They are not venomous, and shouldn't be a problem for walkers, as they will generally move quickly out of the way. There are lizards in many places, and frogs wherever there is access to water. Spring and early summer are good times to see plenty of butterflies, while in some low-lying places mosquitoes might occasionally prove annoying.

NATIONAL PARK

Many maps of Sardinia show the outline of an extensive *parco nazionale*, or national park, encompassing the broad-shouldered schist mountains of Gennargentu, the Supramonte and the rugged limestone uplands and coast of Ogliastra. There was a plan to designate this area as a national park, but it came to nothing, so the lines drawn boldly on so many maps

Lizards are abundant and often take advantage of open areas to sun themselves

are meaningless. There is no doubt that the area deserves protection, but many of the *comunes*, and people whose livelihood depended on the land, opposed the plan, fearing that their rights would be restricted. Graffiti slogans – 'no al parco' ('no to the park') – appeared in many places and can still be seen today.

GETTING TO SARDINIA

Flights

Few direct flights operate between Britain and Sardinia, especially in the winter months. Most flights serve Cagliari, in the south of the island, and Olbia, in the north – either of which can be used to access the area covered by this guidebook. Rather fewer serve Alghero, and this airport is the most remote from the routes in this guide. Airlines include Easyjet www.easyjet.com, Ryanair www.ryanair.com, Jet2 www.jet2.com, BMI Baby www.bmibaby.com and British Airways www.ba.com. If the little airport at Arbatax is developed in the future, it would offer immediate access to the bulk of the walks covered in this book. At the time of writing, it is served from Rome by Meridiana www.meridiana.it.

Ferries

There are useful ferryports at Cagliari and Olbia, with links to Italian ports, and most ferries are operated by Moby Lines www.moby.it and Tirrenia www.tirrenia.it. The occasional ferry from the Italian town of Civitavecchia to Arbatax, leading directly to the area covered by this guidebook, is operated by Tirrenia. There are other ports and operators, and sailings from France and Spain, but these are less useful as they berth too far from the area covered by this guidebook.

GETTING AROUND SARDINIA

Car hire

Cars can be hired on arrival in Sardinia, and it has to be said that cars offer the easiest and most convenient approach to many of the walks in this guidebook. However, some walking routes are linear, and a car is less useful, unless drop-offs and pick-ups can be arranged. If hiring a car, be warned that some of the roads used to reach walking routes are long, lonely, narrow and bendy. In other words, it takes time to get to and from some walks, and it therefore makes more sense to be based in a number of villages near a selection of the routes than to drive long distances from a single base (see 'Where to stay', below).

By law, drivers must have their licences with them at all times, so don't ever leave yours behind at your lodgings. Road rescue (ICA) can be contacted by dialling 116. The driving distance between Olbia and Cagliari is about 300km (186 miles), using the SS125 road. At least 100km (62 miles) has to be travelled from either place before any of the routes in this guidebook can be accessed.

The village of Taquisara flares into life in the summer when the Trenino Verde arrives (Walk 33)

Trains

The layout of Sardinia's railways is simple, and journeys between some towns can be covered effectively and enjoyably. However, the rail network is little use for reaching the area covered by this guidebook. Although there is a railway station at Nuoro, anyone trying to catch a train from Cagliari or Olbia will be told quite bluntly to catch a bus instead. In the middle of summer, a couple of incredibly convoluted mountain railways operate, known as the Trenino Verde. These are best enjoyed by railway enthusiasts, and while they are immensely scenic and enjoyable, they are too slow and infrequent to be of use to walkers.

Buses

Buses allow all towns and most villages within the area covered by this guidebook to be reached, and the author used them effectively while researching this guide. However, anyone relying exclusively on buses needs dedication, as the system is not easily understood. Timetables are almost impossible to get hold of once you are in the area. Even at the main bus stations, details are scanty at best, and you will struggle to get hold of anything useful.

Buses often run from early in the day until late, surprisingly regularly in some places and less frequently in others (maybe only once a day, and perhaps not at all some days).

You need to know the level of provision before you reach the area, and the only place to locate the information you need is the main bus website – Azienda Regionale Sarda Trasporti (ARST) www.arst.sardegna.it. Information is available only in Italian, and it is a struggle to figure out how the site works, but be assured that all the fine detail about routes and timetables is there. Once again, you will not get this level of detailed information once you reach Sardinia, so print out everything you need.

ARST buses are dark blue, and in some areas there are also light-blue FdS buses. The latter are technically part of the railway system, but are effectively merged with ARST. Bus stations (*stazione dei pullman*) exist in towns, while villages and country roads have bus stops (*fermata*). In case of difficulty finding a bus stop, ask a local person for help. Bus drivers may not be keen to pick up or drop passengers off between stops, but may do so on request. Make it quite obvious from the roadside if you want a bus to stop, making sure that there is a safe space to pull over. Be sure to give the driver advance notice if you want to get off the bus in a remote place.

Tickets (*biglietti*) are exceptionally good value, but must be bought before boarding a bus, usually from bars or tobacconists. Again, ask a local person for help to locate a sales outlet. Tickets must be validated by machine on boarding buses, although sometimes the driver does this. If a ticket cannot be bought in advance, bus drivers may sell one on board at an inflated price, or they may insist, with obvious ill-feeling, that passengers get off the bus at a sales outlet further along the route and buy a ticket.

Notes on timetables may include the following terms – *da X per X* (from X to X), *per X da X* (to X from X), *giornaliero* (daily), *feriale* (Monday to Saturday), *scolastico* (schooldays), *domenica/festivo* (Sunday/holiday) and *con cambio a X* (change at X). If you don't understand specific terms, ask someone for an explanation long before you need to catch a bus.

Large towns have their own bus companies running frequent urban services. These include CTM at Cagliari, ASPO at Olbia and ATP at Nuoro. Tickets must be obtained before boarding buses and validated on boarding. They are good value, generally allowing unlimited travel for a period of 90 minutes.

Taxis

In some instances, where buses are infrequent or absent, and car hire is unavailable, a taxi might be sought. Unfortunately, taxis are extremely rare outside the main towns and resorts, and while they seem good value for short urban journeys, they are prohibitively expensive for long journeys into remote areas. Bear in mind that some companies that offer trekking tours are willing to provide lifts to and from the places they regularly take their clients (there are lots of posters advertising these tours – just give the company a ring for more information).

ACCOMMODATION

Despite the apparent remoteness of some mountain villages, a range of accommodation is often available in a surprising number of places. Tourist information offices carry annually updated accommodation booklets, listing everything from hotels and guest-houses to hostels and camp-sites. Listings can be checked online – for Nuoro www.provincia.nuoro.it on the 'Turismo' link, followed by 'Guida

Pointing out a route along the coastline of Ogliastra

all'Ospitalità'; and for Ogliastra www. turismo.ogliastra.it on the 'Dove Dormire' link. Interestingly, the English term 'Bed and Breakfast' features abundantly on roadside notices, although that is no guarantee that the proprietors will speak any English. If a wide range of walks from this guide-book are to be covered effectively, it is probably necessary to stay at a number of locations around the area in order to avoid spending too long travelling.

Of particular note is The Lemon House, a guest-house at Lotzoraì run by Peter Herold and Anne McGlone www.peteranne.it. They offer particular assistance to outdoor enthusiasts, covering such diverse activities as walking, rock-climbing, cycling, kayaking and general touring. They can help, if necessary, with guiding and accompanying their guests and with language issues. Walkers without cars have access to several bus routes at Lotzoraì, and the couple regularly offer guests lifts to and from nearby routes and attractions.

HEALTH AND SAFETY

Visitors are unlikely to contract any illness in Sardinia that they couldn't get at home. (Some low-lying parts of Sardinia used to be malarial, but the island was sprayed with DDT after the Second World War and the disease was eradicated.) All towns and many villages have pharmacies that can provide over-the-counter relief and remedies. More serious illness or injury might require a doctor or hospital treatment, so, if you are a European citizen, carry a European Health Insurance Card, which will allow at least some of the cost of treatments to be recovered.

The island's wildlife should cause few problems. Mosquitoes remain, and, while irritating at times, they carry no harmful diseases. There are snakes, although these will usually slip away when disturbed and will not bite unless cornered or handled. Honeybees will react aggressively towards anyone getting too close to hives, so give a wide berth to any hives you might see.

Flocks of sheep are often guarded by large white dogs that bark menacingly when approached. These are related to Pyrenean sheepdogs, and

work unsupervised by man. They are extremely loyal to their flocks, living and travelling full-time with them. These dogs are not dangerous, provided that they are treated properly. Do nothing to alarm the sheep, as the dogs will interpret this as a threat and will react accordingly. Do not threaten the dogs by shouting or waving arms or sticks. If a dog approaches you, stand absolutely still and keep calm and quiet. The dog is simply trying to identify whether you are a 'threat', and while it may bark, it will not attack without provocation. Once the dog is satisfied that you pose no threat, it will return to the flock. Do not attempt to pet, feed or distract it in any way. It is a working dog whose first responsibility is to the flock it guards.

Sheepdogs often guard flocks, and it is important not to aggravate or threaten them

Travel insurance can be useful, but check the wording of the policy, since some might class mountain walking in Sardinia as a 'hazardous pursuit'. Mountain rescue is available and is provided free of charge (see 'Emergencies', page 32).

FOOD AND DRINK

Surprisingly, for a large Mediterranean island, Sardinia is not noted for seafood. However, sea urchins, or *ricci*, are firm favourites around Cagliari, and fish are featuring more and more on menus. The reason for the dearth of seafood is historical. The cliff coast lacked natural harbours in many places, and accessible stretches of coast were subject to pirate attacks. As the coast was also malarial, settlers gravitated inland towards the mountains.

Cows, sheep and goats provide meat, and most of their milk is used for a variety of cheeses. Ricottas, provolas and pecorinos are Sardinian specialities. Arborea, an old name for Sardinia, is the brand name for local cow's milk. Pigs are widespread, often free range, and a roast suckling pig forms the centrepiece of parties around the island. Pork is used in salamis, hams and other products. Wild boars, rarely seen by walkers, are hunted in the forests. Horse-meat occasionally features on menus. Vegetarians will struggle to find a variety of meat-free items on menus.

Sardinian meals have courses named in the same way as Italian meals, and while some foodstuffs are instantly recognisable, others may be unfamiliar. Anything that is currently in season will be described as *stagione*. Local wines are derived from cannonau grapes, while the name of the local weak beer, Ichnusa, harks back to an ancient name for the island of Sardinia, meaning 'footprint'.

Appetisers, or *antipasta*, often include crispy, poppadum-like *pane carasau*, along with a mixed plate of hams, salamis, pecorino and olives. A thicker crisp-bread, *pistoccu*, is likely to be served if the first course is a broth. Dip the bread into the broth, or into olive oil containing tomato, garlic and basil, to soften it.

The first course, *primi*, commonly includes ravioli-like *culurgionis*, containing pecorino and potato. Also popular is *malloreddus* (often likened to gnocchi, but different), commonly served with sausage and tomato sauce. Spaghetti is also frequently on the menu.

The *secondi*, or main course, is usually spit-roast meat or offal, served on a wooden platter with perhaps no more accompaniment than a scattering of herbs, a little salad or a few fava beans. It could be pig-, goat-, or horse-meat, or even a lamb's head, in which case the brains provide the greatest nourishment!

For *dolci*, or dessert, large ravioli-like, deep-fried, sweet *sebadas* may be produced. A selection of small cakes or biscuits will usually contain almonds. Ricotta may be served.

A good track, flanked by cistus bushes, enters a forest and gradually climbs uphill (Walk 28)

Coffee may be served at the close of a meal, but, more importantly, highly alcoholic *grappa* or *mirto* may be offered. As they say in Sardinia, 'no mirto, no party', and it would be an insult to refuse it!

The author enjoyed a particularly fine, typically Sardinian meal at the Sant' Efisio restaurant near Lotzoraì, www.hotel-santefisio.com, located close to several of the walking routes in this guidebook.

LANGUAGE

Italian is widely spoken and understood around Sardinia, but bear in mind that the native island language, Sard, which is quite distinct from Italian, is also widely spoken. Sard comes in many dialects, which vary remarkably from place to place around the island. Common place-names on maps are in Sard (see Appendix 2 for a glossary of topographical terms) and vary widely in spelling, depending on the dialect. English is often spoken by people working in popular tourist locations and large hotels, but is rarely spoken in rural and mountainous areas of the island. A few basic Italian phrases go a long way (see Appendix 2), and in most places people are remarkably patient while dealing with visitors whose command of the language is limited.

MONEY MATTERS

The Euro is the currency of Sardinia. Large denomination Euro notes are difficult to use for small purchases, so avoid the €500 and €200 notes altogether, and the €100 notes if you can. The rest – €50, €20, €10 and €5 – are the most useful. Coins come in €2 and €1. Small denomination coins come in values of 50c, 20c, 10c, 5c, 2c and 1c. Banks and/or ATMs are often available even in remote mountain villages. Many accommodation providers will accept major credit and debit cards, but be ready to pay cash just in case they don't.

COMMUNICATIONS

Post offices are located in towns and large villages, but may not be available in small villages. Public telephones are also available wherever there are settlements, but if not, ask at a bar. Mobile phone signals are usually good around settlements, but the nature and remoteness of the countryside usually ensures that there are plenty of dead areas where signals cannot be accessed. There are very few internet outlets, but some accommodation providers may offer a service. If access is needed, enquire before booking. (Curiously, the internet service provider Tiscali was named after a remote Sardinian archaeological site.)

TOURIST INFORMATION

Tourist information for the whole of Sardinia is available at www.sardegna turismo.it. Two regional tourism bodies

cover the area featured in this guidebook, Nuoro www.provincia.nuoro.it and Ogliastra www.turismo.ogliastra. it. Tourist information offices are rarely encountered while travelling around such a remote area, but can be found in towns and larger villages. Offices in the following locations may prove useful when looking for information about accommodation and local attractions.

- Nuoro, Piazza Italia, tel 0784-238878
- Oliena, Piazza Berlinguer, tel 0784-286078
- Dorgali, Via Lamarmora, tel 0784-96243
- Cala Gonone, Viale Bue Marino, tel 0784-93696
- Santa Maria Navarrese, Piazza Principessa, tel 0782-614037
- Tortolì, Via Mazzini, tel 0782-622824
- Meana Sardo, Via Montebello, tel 0784-64179
- Aritzo, Via Umberto, tel 0784-627235
- Desulo, Via Lamarmora, tel 338-2501654
- Fonni, Via Zunnui, tel 0784-57197

WALKING IN SARDINIA

In many respects, Sardinia is ideal for walking, while in other respects it is very challenging. It all depends on your expectations and skills. Some paths are notoriously difficult

How to operate a rustic 'gate' in a tall fence

to locate and follow, and even some popular paths are surprisingly rugged. On the other hand, several paths and tracks have been cleared, signposted and waymarked in recent years for the benefit of walkers. In this guidebook the box at the start of each route gives a brief description of the terrain and indicates whether any part of the route is waymarked. It is important to read the route descriptions carefully and to choose routes that suit your desires and abilities.

The cliff coast of Ogliastra is absolutely stunning, but the only route along it, from Santa Maria to Cala Gonone, is the Selvaggio Blu www.selvaggioblu.it. This requires rock-climbing and abseiling skills, and is not included in this guidebook. Some routes offer beach access, while other routes explore further inland on the Supramonte, even to the highest mountains on the island on Gennargentu.

WHERE TO STAY

Sardinia is a large island, and although this guidebook covers only one part of it, walkers wishing to complete several routes would be advised to choose more than one base in which to stay, in order to limit time spent travelling to and from the walks. Some small towns and villages offer access to several walks (see the 'Location of walks' map at the front of the guide to spot concentrations of walks and handy villages).

It is likely that most walkers using this guidebook will arrive via Cagliari, Olbia or Alghero. Nuoro, however, is the largest town lying close to the highest mountains, and it could be used as a base for several days, especially by walkers relying on bus services (remember to obtain and study timetables well in advance). Other useful bases with good access to a handful of walks include Oliena and Dorgali, for the Supramonte and Ogliastra. Villages such as Baunei, Santa Maria, Lotzorai and Tortolì are popular with people exploring Ogliastra. Mountain villages offering accommodation close to walking routes include Ulassai and Laconi. The highest mountains of Gennargentu can be reached easily from Aritzo, Desulo, Tonara and Fonni.

WHAT TO TAKE

Those visiting Sardinia in winter and hoping to explore extensively in the mountains will occasionally need full winter kit, even to the extent of using an ice axe and crampons. For most of the year, however, decent sun protection and lightweight waterproofs to guard against occasional showers are sufficient. In many areas, and particularly in the summer, sources of water dry up, and it is necessary to carry plenty of water to guard against dehydration. Footwear is very much a personal choice, but bear in mind that while some routes follow roads and gravel tracks, others follow very rugged paths or even cross bare, broken and loose rock that may reduce walkers, quite literally, onto their hands and knees!

WHEN TO GO

Sardinia's weather is typically Mediterranean, with long, hot summers and most of the rainfall concentrated in the winter months. Most visiting tourists head for the beaches, which may experience as many as 300 sunny days per year. Many walkers also head for the coast and so will enjoy the same weather.

The mountains are rather different and make their own weather. In winter the highest mountains are covered in snow, sometimes from November until March, to the extent that a couple of small ski pistes flourish briefly. They may also be covered in low cloud, which robs visitors of extensive views. When the coast becomes oppressively hot in summer, the mountains offer cooler conditions

Snow covers the gap of Arcu Gennargentu before the final climb onto Punta La Marmora (Walk 39)

and shady forests. Spring offers some of the best weather and most colourful scenes.

Sardinia occasionally suffers storms and short, but intense periods of heavy rainfall, generally between October and April. Devastating floods in November 2008 caused extensive damage to roads, bridges, houses, tracks and paths. Some of the walking routes in this guidebook run along riverbeds that are normally dry, but occasionally carry torrential floodwater. After heavy rain, therefore, some routes cannot be used. Weather forecasts can be checked out on www.ilmeteo.it.

New signposts give detailed directions throughout a network of waymarked walking trails

WAYMARKING AND ACCESS

While some land is privately owned in Sardinia, many wild areas are held in common and administered by various comunes, or municipal authorities. For the most part there is no objection to walkers following paths and tracks through such places, but bear in mind that activities such as hunting (mainly September to January) take place on this land. In some areas, notably

around the Golgo plateau, local shepherds would prefer visitors to hire them as guides, and to 'encourage' this to happen they aren't keen for paths to be signposted or waymarked. In other places, notably those extensive areas managed by the Sardinian forestry agency, access is actively promoted, and routes have been identified, cleared, marked and signposted (these are mainly concentrated in the area covered by this guide). The trails range from short circular routes to long-distance routes.

MAPS OF SARDINIA

Government maps covering Sardinia are part of the Carta Topografica d'Italia series, published by the

Until recently, few routes were waymarked, but some directions were literally carved in stone

Instituto Geografico Militare d'Italia (IGMI). There are two scales – the 1:50,000 'Serie 50' has orange covers, while the 1:25,000 'Serie 25' has blue covers. Every 'Serie 50' map is divided into quarters to create 'Serie 25' coverage. Bear in mind that some coastal sheets cover very little land area. Sheet-by-sheet coverage can be checked online at www.igmi.org/ware, but the site is available only in Italian – and while it is very useful, it isn't obvious how to get the most out of it. These maps don't show all the available paths and tracks, but other useful maps highlighting at least some useful walking routes are available (see below).

IGMI maps can be ordered in advance from The Map Shop, 15 High Street, Upton-upon-Severn, WR8 0HJ, tel 01684 593146, www.themapshop.co.uk.

Vast areas are managed by Ente Foreste delle Sardegna, the Sardinian forestry agency (www.sardegnaambiente.it/foreste). They have identified, cleared, marked and signposted a series of short and long trails. They publish a series of excellent 1:25,000 scale maps, completely free of charge, covering dozens of waymarked trails. These can be studied online and printed by clicking first on the 'Sentieri' link, then (in spite of everything being only in Italian) clicking on each area, then clicking the 'Scarica la carta' links to find the maps. You won't find better trail maps anywhere on Sardinia.

There is a good 1:50,000 scale map with walking trails highlighted – *Ogliastra* – published by Balzano Edizioni. A similar, but simpler version is published by Edizioni Serinet. Balzano Edizioni also publishes a good 1:50,000 scale *Comunità Montana* map, and sheet 9 covers the mountains around Nuoro. There may be other maps that show walking routes with varying degrees of usefulness and accuracy, but the ones mentioned here are the best.

Travelling around this part of Sardinia requires the use of a suitable road map. Michelin and DeAgostini both publish maps with a good level of detail at a scale of 1:200,000.

EMERGENCIES

Depending on the nature of an emergency, phone for the police (*carabinieri*) on 112, fire service (*vigili del fuoco*) on 115, ambulance (*ambulanza*) on 118, or road rescue (ICA) on 116. There is an organised mountain rescue service on Sardinia, based in Nuoro, with a branch in Urzulei (both in the area covered by this guide). If a rescue is required, call 118 and specify that mountain rescue (*intervento tecnico in montagna*) is needed.

USING THIS GUIDE

This guidebook covers a selection of walking routes stretching from the cliff coast of Ogliastra to the highest mountains of Gennargentu. Routes

The higher parts of the track climb gently around the slopes at Su Arcu Mannu (Walk 43)

include short, easy and popular walks as well as long, difficult and less frequented walks – the information box at the start of each route gives key details about the walk. Always read the route descriptions in advance and don't be tempted to tackle anything beyond your ability.

The routes in the guide are arranged by location – the guide first describes those in the north of the region, then routes further south and east, and subsequently walks in the west. Not all the walks are circular, and for linear routes information on transport back to the start is provided in the route description. Many of the walks adjoin or overlap each other, and can be joined together to create longer walks (the maps show some of the adjoining routes in order to help the reader do this).

Take note of the length of each walk, the time needed to complete it, and the nature of the terrain, then take account of the day's weather. Timings vary from person to person, so if you need more time for one route than that given in the information box, then you will probably need more time for all the routes in the guide. Just work out how much extra time you are likely to need. Conversely, if you finish early on one route, you might well finish early on all of them, and should take this into account when planning each day's walk. The timings are walking times and do not include time spent resting, stopping for lunch, or in long contemplation.

Macchia-covered hills around Giustizieri are easily explored while following clear tracks (Walk 13)

The strip maps in the guidebook concentrate on features close to the walking routes, and if you want to explore further you will need maps extending beyond the area covered. The more remote the route, the more important it is to carry extra mapping. Step-by-step route descriptions are given in the guide, and place-names shown in **bold** in the route description also appear on the strip maps, allowing walkers to keep track of progress. Any shops, bars or restaurants along the way are mentioned, otherwise walkers need to be completely self-sufficient. Although some routes include spring-fed water sources, these cannot be guaranteed during a long, hot and dry spell, so always carry sufficient drinking water.

Sardinia is a huge island, and the 50 walking routes in this guidebook, covering around 750km (465 miles), represent only a fraction of what is available. After completing several routes, walkers should have a good understanding of the nature of the Sardinian landscape, and should be able to approach other parts of the island with greater confidence.

WALK 1
Monte Ortobene from Nuoro

Distance	16km (10 miles)
Start/finish	Chiesa la Solitudine, Nuoro
Total ascent/descent	650m (2130ft)
Time	5hrs
Map	IGMI 'Serie 50' 500, 'Serie 25' 500 IV
Terrain	Roads and tracks, from farmland to wooded slopes, and a steep wooded path for the descent
Refreshment	Plenty of choice in Nuoro; bars on top of Monte Ortobene
Transport/access	ATP city buses run between Nuoro and Monte Ortobene
Note	Descent uses waymarked trail 101

Monte Ortobene is a very popular destination for motorists, although plenty of walkers also climb it. Farm and woodland tracks can be linked to approach the busy summit for exceptional views. A winding, waymarked path can be used on a well-wooded descent to return to Nuoro.

Start at a chapel, **Chiesa la Solitudine**, on the outskirts of Nuoro. A small bar and *gelateria* are available, and the walk goes up the road Via Monte Ortobene. When it bends sharp right, go through a gateway and down a concrete track into holm oak woods. Climb gently and turn right down to a picnic site in mixed woodland. Turn left down a track, and left again at a junction down to the road. Turn right and quickly right again, following a track running parallel to the road for a while. Cross a bridge and pass a turning signposted 'Chiesa di N S di Valverde'. ▶

If visiting the chapel, return here afterwards.

The road reaches a 'Km2' sign at **Janna Ventosa**. Turn right and go through the middle of three gateways. A track descends steeply, then more gently past pines and eucalyptus, while the slopes of Monte

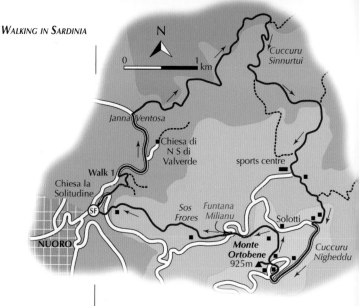

Ortobene are dotted with granite tors. Climb a bit then continue down the track, across bouldery slopes of scrub woodland. Cross a stream-bed and climb gently, through a gateway and over a rise. The tallest trees are cork oaks, then the track climbs past olives, steepening and passing a ruin. The climb continues relentlessly on **Cuccuru Sinnurtui**, with dense macchia, cork oaks and pines alongside.

Turn left at a junction, undulating among mixed woodlands. Stay on the main track, avoiding all others to left and right, and later climb a concrete track with a power line alongside. A derelict **sports centre** stands to the right, around 700m (2300ft). Turn left along a road to reach a turning space beside a weed-grown sports pitch. Continue along and down a track into woods, then climb and watch for a vague path on the right. ◄

If you climb too far a grotesque outcrop is seen, with a gateway alongside. Go back down and look more carefully for the path.

The path is narrow and brambly, then clearer as it climbs through dense woods, a clearing, and more woods. Turn right up a broken concrete track and pass a few properties, reaching a road over 900m (2950ft). Turn left up the road, which curves round **Cuccuru Nigheddu**,

36

offering splendid views, with Monte Bardia to the east, Monte Corrasi south-east, and Gennargentu sprawling south. Reach a couple of restaurants and turn right up a road, then go sharp left up a path to a chapel on a wooded hilltop. Follow a narrow path past a building further along the crest and head down to a car park. (This point is served by ATP buses from Nuoro.)

A pleasant, easy and obvious track runs round the northern slopes of Monte Ortobene

Follow a broad, stone-paved path, rising and falling through the woods. Climb stone steps to the huge bronze statue of Il Redentore ('The Redeemer'), at 925m (3035ft) on **Monte Ortobene**. Enjoy extensive views, marred only by communication masts nearby at 955m (3133ft). Double back to the road and walk round the back of a nearby café/bar called Il Parco. A short concrete track leads onto a winding woodland track. Keep left of a house, passing a corner of a fence, to pick up a path flashed red/white, numbered 101. Walk down through the woods and cross an access track serving a youth centre. Continue down to a derelict building and turn left, almost to a road at **Solotti**, at 820m (2690ft).

Just before reaching the road, turn left through a brambly gap to follow a path. A fence and wall push the path away from the road, while red/white flashes show the way ahead, through a network of paths. An old track leads down to a road, but merely clip a bend and step behind 'arrow' signs to continue down the path. Either cross the road or walk under it at **Funtana Milianu**. Go down granite steps to follow a walled or fenced path that turns right down a steep track then quickly levels out among tall broom. Join a broader track and turn right, in effect straight ahead, to a cross-track where tall pines stand among holm oaks at **Sos Frores**, at 707m (2320ft).

Keep straight ahead, signposted 'La Solitudine', following the path downhill until it rears uphill, worn and grooved. The trail is marked left – it is initially vague (flashed red/white), but becomes clearer as it climbs a groove past outcrops and boulders. Reach a clear track, but don't follow it. Turn quickly right and left to follow a narrow parallel path. Keep straight ahead along a clear path, going over a slight rise then down a groove. Pass between a covered reservoir and a house, walk down a concrete track to a transformer tower, then go straight ahead down a gritty path. Turn left up a road (or squeeze through a narrow bridge beneath), then turn sharp right and walk steeply down a narrow path. Fork left to finish in front of the chapel at **La Solitudine**.

WALK 2
Monte Corrasi from Oliena

Distance	12km (from Coop Enis) or 20km (7½ or 12½ miles)
Start/finish	Oliena
Alternative start/finish	Coop Enis (if arriving by car or taxi – just follow signs to Coop Enis and avoid the road walking)
Total ascent/descent	850 or 1200m (2790 or 3935ft)
Time	4 or 6hrs
Map	IGMI 'Serie 50' 500, 'Serie 25' 500 III
Terrain	A road and track climb high into the mountains, with rugged paths over the highest parts

| Refreshment | Plenty of choice in Oliena; bar at Coop Enis |
| Transport/access | Regular daily buses serve Oliena from Nuoro and Dorgali |

Monte Corrasi is the highest of a formidable group of mountains towering high above Oliena. A winding road and a zigzag track seem to climb for ever on its slopes, allowing steep and rocky mountainsides to be scaled with relative ease. A rugged path crosses the summit and offers extensive views.

Start from the church, Chiesa Santa Maria, around 350m (1150ft) in **Oliena**. Walk through the cobbled Piazza

The vehicle track climbs high above Oliena, offering a relatively easy climb towards Monte Corrasi

39

Santa Maria, up a granite-paved road. Just before the tourist information office, turn left up steps through an amphitheatre to the comune building on Piazza Aldo Moro. Follow the cobbled Via Dr Antonio Puligheddu left of the building and turn left up the steep Salita Agostino Depretis. Climb steps and turn right along Via Ippolito Nievo, then left up Via Monte Grappa to the 'Localita Turistica Monte Maccione' sign. Turn left up Via Maggiore Toselli, and continue straight up Via Corrasi and straight up a concrete road sign-posted 'Coop Enis'.

Pass **Sos Pisches B&B**, over 450m (1475ft), climbing a very bendy concrete road on a steep slope of holm oak, cypress and pines. Pass a small car park at **Coop Enis**, where there is a hotel, bar/restaurant and campsite around 700m (2300ft). Continue along a gravel road, which becomes concrete again, flanked by dense holm oak apart from a little viewpoint. Concrete gives way to gravel, so fork left up a broad path across densely wooded slopes. Join a stone-paved track, turn left to climb, and it reverts to concrete.

The return route joins the outward route here.

Keep left at a junction at **Daddana**. ◄ The concrete track ends at a turning place around a tree. Climb a

40

bendy, stony track, passing stone huts. Holm oaks grow tall and stout on grassy slopes studded with big boulders. Follow the most obvious track as it winds uphill, supported by buttresses, with ever-expanding views. Steep limestone slopes feature amazing buttresses and pinnacles, then the track reaches a turning space at **Scala 'e Pradu**, at 1227m (4026ft).

Here four paths branch apart, and the one for Monte Corrasi is the furthest right, passing a little shrine. Follow it into a dip, where there is a sheepfold down to the left. The path is clear as it climbs a rocky, stone-strewn slope with tufts of matted vegetation. Cross a rise and drop a little, then climb more steeply, passing rocky stumps. A vegetated groove climbs between rocks, past a few hawthorns, with a bouldery slope and steep, rugged terrain beyond. Level out, climb another rocky, stone-strewn slope, then level out on a grassy shoulder. The path splits, and while this isn't obvious, it is important.

A well-worn path heads right, climbing to the bare limestone summit of **Monte Corrasi**, at 1463m (4800ft). The views from its abrupt edge are extensive, stretching

Looking back to the bare rock slopes of Monte Corrasi on the descent to Scala 'e Marras

41

This path becomes significantly tougher, so if in doubt, retrace your steps to Coop Enis and Oliena.

east to the mountains of Ogliastra and the coast, sweeping north and far inland beyond Nuoro, then west and south to the Gennargentu massif. Walk back down to the grassy shoulder and turn right along the other path, watching for cairns to confirm it. ◀

The path leads down through a vegetated cleft in the mountainside. Walk through it and later climb from it, picking a way carefully down a rocky, stone-strewn slope. Admire the amazing rugged scenery, but also watch for cairns, and take special care to avoid the rocky ridge. Pass beneath the boughs of a prominent tree, then almost level out to follow a broad, rocky part of the ridge. Looking back, Monte Corrasi appears as a perfect cone. Follow the path until it drops again and the cone passes from sight.

Take care to spot the path swinging right across the crest at **Scala 'e Marras**, around 1250m (4100ft). There is a glimpse back to the cone, while a cairn confirms the route. This sharp right turn is on bare limestone, then the path slices across the western slopes on a falling traverse. Rocky, stony slopes give way to holm oak woods with clearings. One steep descent is followed by a short climb, otherwise the path is narrow and occasionally vague. Keep watching for cairns and later drop onto a track.

Turn right, gently rising and falling as the track crosses a slope of holm oak and arbutus, with rock towers and buttresses high above. A narrow path leads onwards, rising and falling across a steep, crumbling, wooded slope and crossing a boulder-jam below Monte Corrasi. A wire fence leads onwards and the path drops to a track. Turn right to walk up it, passing a spring in a dip. The track climbs across a mountain pasture dotted with trees, and later runs downhill at **Daddana**. Reach a bend on a concrete track followed earlier in the day, turn left and retrace steps to **Coop Enis** or **Oliena** to finish.

WALK 3
Punta Ortu Camminu and Sos Nidos

Distance	21km (13 miles)
Start/finish	Oliena or Coop Enis
Total ascent/descent	1250m (4100ft)
Time	7hrs
Map	IGMI 'Serie 50' 500, 'Serie 25' 500 III
Terrain	A road and track climb high into the mountains, with very rough and rocky ground on the highest parts. A steep and stony descent into woods.
Refreshment	Plenty of choice in Oliena; bar at Coop Enis
Transport/access	Regular daily buses serve Oliena from Nuoro and Dorgali

These two mountains can be reached directly from Oliena following the same winding road and track used for the initial part of the ascent of Monte Corrasi (Walk 2). However, the slopes are rocky and largely pathless, and this walk is for sure-footed walkers only. If the full circuit is followed, note that the descent is particularly rugged and requires great care.

Start by following Walk 2 to climb from **Oliena**. (For those walking the full circuit there is little to be gained by driving up to **Coop Enis**, but it is an alternative start point for those intending to retrace their steps from the summits.) Follow Walk 2 all the way up to the turning space at **Scala 'e Pradu**, at 1227m (4026ft).

Here four paths branch apart, and the one for Punta Ortu Camminu is the furthest left. This path drops to a small wire-fenced enclosure, so leave it and pick any likely looking line uphill. Walk on angled rock slabs, rather than wiry macchia. Clear weather helps enormously with route choices, and the higher parts, while rocky in places, are surprisingly grassy in others. Cross a slight gap to

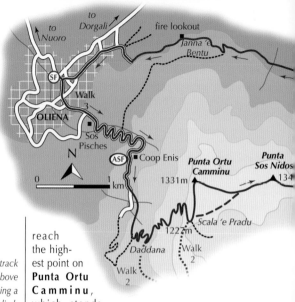

The vehicle track climbs high above Oliena, offering a relatively easy climb onto Punta Ortu Camminu

reach the highest point on **Punta Ortu Camminu**, which stands at 1331m (4367ft) and bears a square cairn. There are extensive views.

There are cliffs to the west and north, so descend east towards a broad gap. Again, walk on angled slabs rather than macchia. The gap is above 1200m (3935ft) and a rocky slope beyond leads onto the prominent dome of **Punta Sos Nidos**, rising to 1348m (4422ft). From here, enjoy views of the limestone mountains of Ogliastra and the more distant granite whalebacks of Gennargentu. (It is possible to return directly to Scala 'e Pradu from here, picking up a line of cairns and a path, without having to climb back over Punta Ortu Camminu.)

The next stage is rocky, pathless and needs great care. Head south-east from the summit and keep away from cliff edges. The overall aim is to head roughly eastwards, watching carefully for good lines that allow feet to 'stick' to steep limestone, passing occasional juniper bushes. At first it isn't possible to stay high on the ridge, but later the ridge provides the best line. (Local shepherds run along this ridge!) The most awkward footwork comes between two holm oak trees – the only ones on the crest. When dense juniper is reached, the rocky crest splits and two ridges run down to a grassy gap. Walk down a little valley in between, using a vague path. The gap stands at almost 950m (3115ft), and provides immediate access to **Punta Cusidore** (see Walk 4).

Turn left to leave the gap, where two thin paths soon join to form one vague, stony path winding down between juniper bushes. Watch for little cairns, keeping away from the cliffs of Punta Cusidore on the right, but don't go down the valley on the left either. A bar of rock pushes the path towards the valley. However, watch for cairns and follow a vague path down a steep, rocky slope. Keep the valley on the left and a scree slope on the right. The path and scree later descend as one steep, cha-otic mass of rock and rubble into dense woods of holm

Turn right here
if descending to
Monserrata, the start
of Walk 4.

oak and juniper. Watch for a cairn to enter the woods correctly, and follow the path until a huge limestone outcrop is reached at **Preda 'e Littu**, at 335m (1099ft). ◄

Turn left gently down a track, crossing rocky bumps, followed by a series of gradual ascents, with views of the mountains and cultivated lowlands wherever the trees are short. Keep straight ahead when another track drops right, and fork left uphill soon afterwards. Keep climbing, with fewer views, among tall holm oak and arbutus. Level out with a view of Monte Ortobene ahead, while Punta Cusidore lies behind. Climb again, level out, and bend left and right to reach a broad firebreak on a shoulder. Pass a fire lookout at **Janna 'e Bentu**, from where there are splendid views from Oliena to Monte Ortobene and along a broad, cultivated valley towards the coast.

Follow the track onwards, downhill and undulating, to the end of the firebreak. Reach a junction beside a few vines and keep right to pass a building, then turn right downhill, then go left and level out, following a road ahead and up into **Oliena**. Turn left at a junction and go up Via Masiloghi to a cobbled road, passing the church of San Francesco. Go through a cobbled crossroads and down the narrow Via Guiseppe Garibaldi. Fork right at a gable-end poetic mural and almost immediately go through a tiny crossroads and along Via Eleonora d'Arborea. This leads to Piazza Santa Maria, where a right turn leads to the church of Chiesa Santa Maria.

WALK 4

Punta Cusidore from Nostra Signora di Monserrata

Distance	13km (8 miles)
Start/finish	Nostra Signora di Monserrata
Total ascent/descent	1000m (3280ft)
Time	5hrs
Map	IGMI 'Serie 50' 500, 'Serie 25' 500 III

Terrain	Easy roads and tracks on cultivated and wooded slopes give way to steep scree and steeper rock, requiring hands-on scrambling
Refreshment	Bar beside the main road near the church
Transport/access	Regular daily buses pass the church from Nuoro, Oliena and Dorgali. Given due notice, buses will stop on the road between Oliena and Dorgali, near the turning for Santuario Nostra Signora di Monserrata, around 150m (490ft). Car parking at the church.

Punta Cusidore rises prominently from the road between Oliena and Dorgali. Its pale rocky peak towers above dense evergreen slopes. Punta Cusidore is really the preserve of rock climbers, though this route allows confident walkers to reach the peak. Paths used for the ascent get progressively steeper, and scrambling skills are necessary to reach the summit.

Walk up the concrete road serving the church of **Nostra Signora di Monserrata**, but turn left along another road. (If you have parked at the church, walk back down the road and turn right.) The road soon bends right, then keep right at a later junction. Follow the road uphill, with eucalyptus alongside, and turn left at a junction, gently undulating past fields and vineyards. When the road turns left, keep straight ahead along a track. This later turns right, climbing steep and straight towards dense woods. Turn right at a junction beside a couple of large boulders. The track mostly rises, reaching a huge limestone outcrop, **Preda 'e Littu**, at 335m (1099ft).

47

Turn left up a path through dense holm oak and juniper. Emerge onto a steep scree slope and pick a way up a chaotic mass of rock and rubble. As height is gained, get off the scree onto a firm, steep and rocky slope. Watch for cairns and follow a vague path, with the scree and cliffs of Punta Cusidore to the left and a valley down to the right. Cross a bar of rock and keep watching for cairns, which reveal a vague and stony path winding up between juniper bushes. The path splits at a higher level, but both lines lead to a grassy gap at almost 950m (3115ft).

Drift left and pick up a path across a slope of macchia, with cliffs rising above. Keep an eye on the cliffs, as there is only one breach that ordinary walkers can scramble through to gain the higher slopes. Watch for cairns and climb up a tongue of scree. Scramble up steep rock slabs, looking ahead for cairns, but also looking back to remember details for the descent. Another tongue of scree leads up to much steeper bare rock. Aim for what appears to be a cleft between twin peaks of rock, but only climb this if you are certain you can do it in reverse. Above and beyond is the rocky summit of **Punta Cusidore**, at 1147m

Take great care scrambling onto Punta Cusidore, which gets progressively more difficult with height

(3763ft). Enjoy extensive views, then retrace your steps
faithfully to Nostra Signora di Monserrata. Alternatively,
use the latter half of Walk 3 to Oliena.

WALK 5
Tiscali from Valle di Lanaittu

Distance	7km (4½ miles)
Start/finish	Casa Buduraí, Valle di Lanaittu
Total ascent/descent	250m (820ft)
Time	3hrs
Map	IGMI 'Serie 50' 500, 'Serie 25' 500 II and III
Terrain	Easy woodland tracks, then steep and rocky paths, with some hands-on scrambling
Refreshment	Possibly at Casa Buduraí
Transport/access	Casa Buduraí is 8km (5 miles) from a bus route; car parking at Casa Buduraí

Many walkers set out for Tiscali, but not all of them
make it, getting lost in a labyrinth of woodland
tracks and paths. Route-finding is easiest if an
approach is made from Casa Buduraí in the Valle
di Lanaittu. This walk to Tiscali is short, leaving time
to explore the many other features of interest along
the way.

Valle di Lanaittu
Signposted off the approach road to Valle di Lanaittu
are a resurgent river and parkland at Su Gologone
(entry charge), and the caves of Grotta Rifugio and
Grotta del Guano. Notices beside the dirt road indi-
cate points of interest in the valley, while signposts
point the way to Casa Buduraí and Rifugio Sa Ohe.
Most people drive to Sa Ohe, where there is access to
Grotta Sa Ohe and the nuraghic villages of Sa Sedda

and Sos Carros (entry charges). Attempting to reach Tiscali from Sa Ohe involves navigating a maze of woodland tracks and paths. The approach from Casa Buduraí is simpler.

From **Casa Buduraí** continue along the dirt road almost to a boulder-paved ford. Turn left just before it, following a track that meanders and undulates, running into woodland and crossing the riverbed a few times. It generally climbs gently, and passes a point where the return route from Tiscali comes in from the left. Keep right on the track, climbing short and steep, then follow a long, gentle, straight ascent to a clearing where there is a peculiar junction of tracks and paths.

Turn left up a track which is rocky underfoot, used by 4WD vehicles to get people closer to Tiscali. The track bends left and right, then there is a parking space on the left for vehicles. The track ahead becomes a broad and stony path, climbing and turning quickly left and right. Climb steeply ahead and watch carefully on the right to spot an old juniper trunk bearing faded paint marks. Turn left, straight up a steep and narrow path, from a wooded slope onto a rocky slope. Climb up scree and climb past boulders.

Turn left into a boulder-jam, where a huge rock tower has split from a cliff. Use hands to get up through a cleft and down the other side. Continue along a rock terrace, often walking beneath an overhang. The rock underfoot becomes awkward, but the way ahead remains clear. Take care not to fall into a monstrous hole at **Tiscali**, over 400m (1310ft), but keep left of it and pick a way round the rocky rim to find the entrance to the cave.

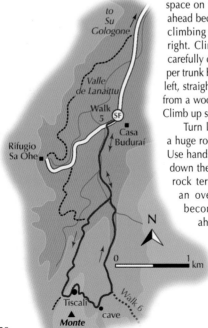

50

Steep and rocky slopes, involving hands-on scrambling, feature on the ascent and descent

Tiscali

Stone steps lead into a collapsed cave (entry charge), containing the crumbling remains of a late nuraghic village. There is evidence that it was built in a hurry and was unable to thrive, suggesting that the builders were on the run, trying to keep out of sight in a remote area with few resources and little water. The internet company Tiscali is named after this place, and was founded by Renato Soru of Sardinia.

Climb out of the cave and use hands to scramble down a steep, rocky, well-worn path, past a small **cave**, to a clearing and a sign. Turn left and walk down through a valley, following a path through woods and along a bouldery riverbed. Keep an eye on the path as it enters and leaves the riverbed over and over again. Eventually, reach a junction with the track that was followed earlier in the day. Simply turn right and follow the track straight back to **Casa Buduraí**.

WALK 6
Tiscali via Scala de Surtana

Distance	10km (6 miles)
Start/finish	Su Liddone, near Dorgali
Total ascent/descent	480m (1575ft)
Time	4hrs
Map	IGMI 'Serie 50' 500, 'Serie 25' 500 II and III
Terrain	Two steep, rocky paths require hands-on scrambling, and these are separated by an easy woodland path
Refreshment	None
Transport/access	Su Liddone is 10km (6 miles) from a bus route near Dorgali. By car, follow the main road south of Dorgali, past the tunnel mouth for Cala Gonone, and turn right down a zigzag road. Follow this, passing the church of Nostra Signora del Buon Cammino. Reach a car park at Su Liddone, around 175m (575ft), beside the Riu Flumineddu.

The valley of the Riu Flumineddu stretches southwards from Dorgali, and its western flank is one long cliff line. There is a notable breach at Scala de Surtana, and this can be used to reach the celebrated nuraghic village of Tiscali, as an alternative to the approach from Valle di Lanaittu (Walk 5).

From the car park at **Su Liddone** cross the river using boulder stepping stones, walk up a track on the other side and turn left along another track marked 'Tiscali'. Although the track heads upstream, it includes a descent, and the bedrock near the river is granite, giving rise to a gritty surface underfoot. Turn left at a junction of tracks, which is quickly followed by another junction. Go either way here – left is slightly more direct, while right offers the chance to buy cheese from a farm. Shortly after both tracks join again, turn right along another track and take note of a sign detailing entry charges at Tiscali.

The track becomes a narrow path winding uphill between boulders and macchia. As the slope steepens there is plenty of limestone, requiring the use of hands in places. Note the words '**Scala de Surtana**' carved into the rock near the top. This is the only 'easy' route through a long line of cliffs, and it gives access to a gentle valley beyond, at 383m (1257ft). The path is well trodden as it runs through the valley – sometimes with views of cliffs towering above, and sometimes in dense woods. Avoid paths to right and left, which lead to rock-climbing routes. The path descends gently at first, becoming rough and rocky before crossing a stream-bed. After another

The Scala de Surtana is the only breach for walkers trying to reach Tiscali from the Riu Flumineddu

stretch in dense woods, it emerges into a clearing surrounded by rocky peaks.

Turn left, signposted 'Tiscali', up a rocky, stony path to a small **cave** at the base of a cliff. The path swings right to climb further, turning right at a signposted junction. Traverse a rocky slope where junipers grow, then climb a steep, rocky, well-worn path, where small signs assure visitors that **Tiscali** is close to hand. The arrival at the entrance to the late nuraghic cave village, over 400m (1310ft), is quite sudden. ◄ After visiting the site, retrace your steps to **Su Liddone**.

For more information about Tiscali, see Walk 5.

WALK 7
Gola de Su Gorropu

Distance	8km (5 miles) or, finish at Su Liddone, 13km (8 miles)
Start/finish	Genna Silana
Alternative finish	Su Liddone, near Dorgali
Total ascent	80 or 630m (260 or 2065ft)
Total descent	630 or 730m (2065 or 2395ft)
Time	3hrs 30min
Map	IGMI 'Serie 50' 500 and 157, 'Serie 25' 500 II and 517 I
Terrain	Good tracks and paths down a steep slope. Gentle paths and tracks through a well-wooded valley.
Refreshment	Bar at Genna Silana
Transport/access	Infrequent daily buses serve Genna Silana from Dorgali and Tortolí. Su Liddone is 10km (6 miles) from a bus route near Dorgali.

Most walkers visiting the deep, rock-walled gorge of Gola de Su Gorropu follow an unexciting valley track, retracing their steps afterwards. A more scenic approach drops from Genna Silana, although the climb back uphill could be tiring. The best option is to continue down through the valley to Su Liddone, if a pick-up can be arranged.

Start at **Genna Silana**, 1017m (3337ft), where a roadside signpost indicates 'Gola de Su Gorropu'. Walk down a stony track and almost immediately fork left down a path to a fence and stile, entering woods dominated by stout holm oaks. Pass a crude hut and follow a well-trodden path across a rugged slope beneath cliffs, gradually descending to a track. Turn left down the track, which is broad in places, but where the slope is steep and bouldery it narrows to a path. Go in and out of holm oak woods, with views from the open slopes of Costa Silana.

A remarkable leaning tower of rock is passed on the way down to Gola de Su Gorropu

Map continues on page 57

The Flumineddu valley looks gentle from here, with no hint of the dramatic scenery to come.

A sweeping zigzag leads down into holm oak woods, where a pinnettu is passed. The path drops well below cliffs on a steep slope and enters arbutus woods. Emerge from the woods to cross a scree slope and reach the foot of cliffs. Head down past another pinnettu, **Coile 'e or Sedas**, passing close to a limestone pinnacle. The path again descends below the cliffs, winding down through woods. It is easy to follow at first, becomes rugged at the bottom, then is tangled among oleasters when a riverbed is reached below 400m (1310ft).

Cross the rocky riverbed at **Gola de Su Gorropu**, heading upstream at the same time, looking for a trodden path up the other side. ▶

There are now two options – either retrace the outward route to climb back to Genna Silana, which is short and steep, or continue down through the Flumineddu valley to Su Liddone, which is a long and gentle route. Both options take the same time, but the valley path is easier.

It is worth penetrating this awesome deep and rocky gorge, scrambling past huge water-worn boulders, and retracing your steps later.

Extension to Su Liddone (9km/5½ miles)

To continue down the Flumineddu valley, look carefully for the path climbing from the riverbed. Once found, it quickly levels out and runs easily through arbutus woods. The bedrock is no longer limestone, but schist. The path undulates and is gently graded, while the woods become quite mixed and there are areas of macchia. Later, the path rises and falls on granitic bedrock and there are taller trees as a stone-built *funtana* (spring) is passed. The path broadens to a track as it runs downstream roughly parallel to the **Riu Flumineddu**. Some parts are rough and stony, but one ascent is stone-paved, with good views along the valley. Go down a bendy stretch of track, partly surfaced in concrete, and later pass a junction. The continuing track is sandy and gritty underfoot.

Later, if a broken bridge has been replaced, cross it and continue along a road. If not, then continue along the track. Tiscali is signposted to the left (see Walk 6), but keep straight ahead to a fork. Go either way, right being the most direct, while left offers the chance to buy cheese from a **farm**. Both tracks join again, but keep right at the next fork. The track continues downstream, but also climbs. Turn right down to the river and cross it using boulder stepping-stones to reach a car park around 175m (575ft), near **Su Liddone**, where a pick-up should be arranged.

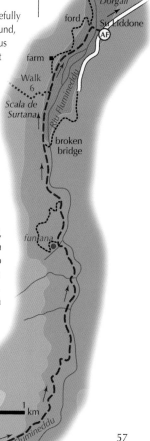

WALK 8

*Dorgali, Monte Bardia and
Cala Gonone*

Distance	11km (6½ miles)
Start	Corso Umberto, Dorgali
Finish	Harbour, Cala Gonone
Total ascent	600m (1970ft)
Total descent	950m (3115ft)
Time	4hrs
Map	IGMI 'Serie 50' 500, 'Serie 25' 500 I and II
Terrain	Easy paths become very rocky and stony, requiring careful route-finding in woodland, with some mild scrambling
Refreshment	Plenty of choice in Dorgali and Cala Gonone
Transport/access	Regular daily buses link Dorgali and Cala Gonone with Nuoro

Monte Bardia towers above Dorgali, and its steep, well-wooded limestone slopes seem impregnable. Fortunately, an old mule track crosses a shoulder and a road crosses a gap, while cairns and chiselled waymarks reveal a rugged path from one side of the mountain to the other.

Start at the top of the main street, Corso Umberto, in **Dorgali**, where Via La Marmora crosses, around 400m (1310ft). Walk straight up Via Mare, swinging right and later turning left up to a by-pass road above town. Turn right down the road, then quickly left up a track marked 'Galleria Vecchia'. Climb steeply, cross a water channel and level out, then climb steeply again. The gradient eases as the track crosses a slope of holm oaks. Look carefully uphill to spot a green pole supporting a power line, then look carefully to spot a stony path climbing steeply up to the pole. A splendid stone-paved mule track zigzags up a cliff face.

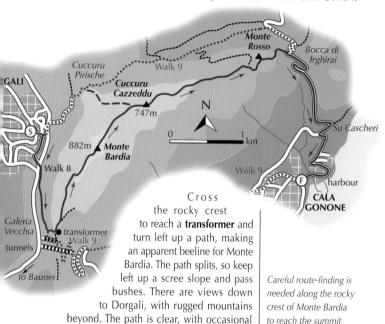

Cross the rocky crest to reach a **transformer** and turn left up a path, making an apparent beeline for Monte Bardia. The path splits, so keep left up a scree slope and pass bushes. There are views down to Dorgali, with rugged mountains beyond. The path is clear, with occasional

Careful route-finding is needed along the rocky crest of Monte Bardia to reach the summit

circle/triangle markers carved on limestone. Cross the rocky crest and watch for cairns and markers over bare rock and scree. Aim towards the rocky summit dome, knowing that the path skirts left of its cliffs. When the base of the cliff is reached, 'XM BARDIA' is carved into the rock.

Turn left beneath the cliff then scramble slowly uphill, watching for cairns, looking for good holds on rock, taking care on scree and among bushes. The path is gentler in dense holm oak woods, meandering and undulating close to the rocky crest. The summit of **Monte Bardia** bears a metal cross at 882m (2894ft). Looking down, Corso Umberto slices through Dorgali, leading the eye west to Monte Ortobene. The nearby limestone mountains of Ogliastra give way to the distant, high, granite and schist mountains of Gennargentu, while a fine stretch of coast is also in view.

Continue along the rocky, wooded crest to descend. The path is rugged, vague in places, marked by cairns and occasional stones lodged in the branches of trees. Proceed slowly, and if the path is lost, turn back and find it. An easier stretch reaches a gap where there are patchy bushes, scree and bare rock. There are two sets of cairns – one set leading left down to Dorgali, if an early descent is required, and another set crossing the gap to climb **Cuccuru Cazzeddu**, passing its summit cairn at 747m (2451ft).

Descend through dense woods, watching carefully for the path. Emerge and keep right of a sprawling rocky hump, following cairns across a rocky slope, going in and out of wooded areas. Climb an easy scree slope, cross a gentle bushy rise, then follow a broad and obvious path making sweeping zigzags downhill. Climb another scree slope and turn right to follow a narrow, cairned path carefully down slopes of honeycombed, fissured, man-eating limestone on **Monte Rosso**. Tread slowly and carefully, and don't lose the way while squeezing past juniper bushes. A hairpin bend is seen on a road below, but don't drop directly to it. Look ahead to spot a clear line of descent, seeing all the way down to the road at **Bocca di Irghirai**, around 300m (985ft).

Turn right to walk down the road to finish at the harbour at **Cala Gonone** (for route details see Walk 9). If you need to return to Dorgali, either catch a bus or use the latter half of Walk 9.

Cala Gonone, where anyone walking out of season can expect to have the beach to themselves

WALK 9
Dorgali and Cala Gonone

Distance	16km (10 miles)
Start/finish	Corso Umberto, Dorgali
Total ascent/descent	900m (2950ft)
Time	5hrs
Map	IGMI 'Serie 50' 500, 'Serie 25' 500 I and II
Terrain	Woodland tracks and paths, with some road-walking
Refreshment	Plenty of choice in Dorgali and Cala Gonone
Transport/access	Regular daily buses link Dorgali and Cala Gonone with Nuoro

There are plenty of roads, tracks and paths on the slopes of Monte Bardia, which can be linked to form a circuit around the mountain – from Dorgali to Cala Gonone and back to Dorgali. The route is easily cut in half as there are bus services between the two towns.

Start at the top of the main street, Corso Umberto, in **Dorgali**, where Via La Marmora crosses, around 400m (1310ft). Walk straight up Via Mare, turning left to the church of Santa Maria Maddalena e Santu Lutziferu. Turn right up a short, steep road with steps alongside, then left along a concrete road. This runs parallel to a by-pass road above town, which is joined further along. Use a pedestrian crossing on the by-pass, turn left, then quickly right as signposted to 'Pirische'. Walk up a concrete road

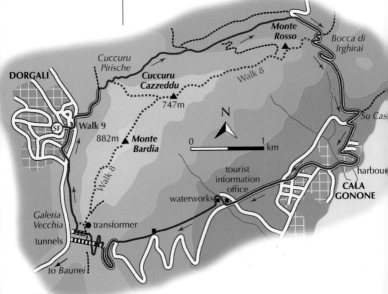

on a slope of leaning pines and holm oaks, turning right when signposted 'Eremu de Santu Lombertu'.

A stony path climbs steeply, worn to bare rock in places. Keep right at a junction and keep climbing, with views back to Dorgali, entering holm oak woods and crossing a shoulder around 550m (1085ft) on **Cuccuru Pirische**. Stay on the main path and avoid lesser ones on either side. Head straight downhill, which is steep and rugged at times, going round occasional bends but avoiding all sharp left turns. At one point, to keep straight ahead you must fork right, climb a little and continue downhill. At the next fork, head left downhill, the route becoming gentle and easy later among holm oak, arbutus and heather.

Turn right up a concrete road which twists and turns, passing through a rock cutting around 300m (985ft) at **Bocca di Irghiriai**. ▸ There is a view down the other side to Cala Gonone, with lots of bare rock, shrubby macchia, juniper, lentisc and euphorbia. Walk down the road and round hairpin bends on steep slopes. There are holm oak trees further down, then dense lentisc as limestone gives way to basalt.

Walk 8 joins here.

A track heads left at **Su Cascheri**, but stay on the road, later turning left to a hotel. Follow the winding Via Marco Polo down to the harbour at **Cala Gonone**. (This popular resort offers all services, including fascinating coastal cruises and buses to Dorgali, Oliena and Nuoro.) Follow a road uphill and inland, turning right just before a church up Viale Colombo. A pine-shaded, black-and-white pavement follows the road, losing the shade while climbing to a roundabout above town. (A bar/restaurant and a tourist information office lie to the right.) Go further up the road to a multi-lingual 'Good Bye to Cala Gonone' sign.

Turn right along a clear track, pass a **waterworks** building and turn sharp left. The track rises and falls, then a right turn reveals a ruler-straight track, climbing steep and stony at times. Holm oaks grow alongside, while areas of bushy macchia allow views back to Cala Gonone. A gentler stretch leads to a small stone building

The return to Dorgali follows an old road through a tunnel, where a torch is not normally required

near a road bend. Keep climbing, steeply at one point, to reach the road again. Follow the road uphill to twin **tunnels**, but don't go through them.

Walk up a broad track, bending left above the tunnels. Count a series of concrete bends – right, left, right – then at the next left, turn right up another track, which immediately forks. Keep left and go gently down through an old tunnel – **Galeria Vecchia**. ◄ Follow a track gently down across a steep and rocky slope, passing cliffs and holm oaks. The track drops steeply, levels out to cross a water channel, then drops steeply to a by-pass above **Dorgali**. Turn right up the road, quickly left down another road, then right to return to the start in the town centre.

A torch isn't necessary, except in the evening.

WALK 10
Genna 'e Petta and Sa Portiscra

Distance	8km (5 miles)
Start/finish	Genna 'e Petta
Total ascent/descent	300m (985ft)
Time	3hrs
Map	IGMI 'Serie 50' 517, 'Serie 25' 517 I
Terrain	A track gives way to a rough and stony path on rocky, wooded slopes
Refreshment	None
Transport/access	Infrequent daily buses serve Genna 'e Petta from Dorgali and Tortolí. By car, if at Genna 'e Petta the gate to Sa Portiscra is open, then cars can be driven 2.5km (1½ miles) along the track.
Note	Route uses waymarked trail 181

If you don't know what a pinnettu is, or a nuraghic village, or a cerv for that matter, then a walk along the Sentiero degli Ovili at Sa Portiscra will set matters straight. This short trail runs through a remote area, but is adequately signposted and waymarked, comprising a descent, short loop and re-ascent.

Genna 'e Petta is a gap at Km187 on the bleak mountain road high above Su Gorropu, at 900m (2950ft). There are two gates beside the road – one for Sa Portiscra, which this walk follows, and the other for a forestry house passed on Walk 11. As a walk, the track is pleasant, rising gently, with increasingly good views beyond scrub woodland slopes. Descend through a cutting, passing stout holm oaks and junipers, with a view along the valley of Codula Luna. The track ends suddenly at **Sa Portiscra**, with wigwam-like pinnettus (shepherds' huts) above and below, while a stone wall topped by a wooden palisade surrounds an enclosure containing cerv or Sardinian deer (office, entry

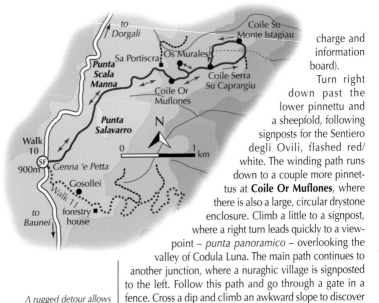

charge and information board).

Turn right down past the lower pinnettu and a sheepfold, following signposts for the Sentiero degli Ovili, flashed red/white. The winding path runs down to a couple more pinnettus at **Coile Or Muflones**, where there is also a large, circular drystone enclosure. Climb a little to a signpost, where a right turn leads quickly to a viewpoint – *punta panoramico* – overlooking the valley of Codula Luna. The main path continues to another junction, where a nuraghic village is signposted to the left. Follow this path and go through a gate in a fence. Cross a dip and climb an awkward slope to discover a mass of inter-connected, circular stone dwellings at **Os Murales**, with a central stone tower. Retrace your steps to the path junction to continue.

∧ *rugged detour allows an exploration of the nuraghic village of Or Murales*

Walk down a stony path, reaching another pinnettu and sheepfold at **Coile Serra Su Caprargiu**, at 710m (2330ft). There are good valley views until the path is swallowed into dense woods further downhill. Pass a signpost at Coile Sa Tuvera, where there is a sheepfold to the right and a pinnettu beyond. The path drops further and crosses a stream-bed around 550m.

Zigzag up to **Coile Su Monte Istagiau**, passing another sheepfold and pinnettu. Follow the path uphill, then descend gently for a bit, then go uphill again, before descending to cross the stream-bed again. Turn left to climb from it, up a well-wooded slope. The path crosses a more open and stony slope and returns to **Coile Serra Su Caprargiu**, at 710m (2330ft). Turn right and retrace your steps back up to **Sa Portiscra** and along the track to finish at **Genna 'e Petta**.

WALK 11
Codula Luna and Cala Gonone

Distance	25km (15½ miles)
Start	Genna 'e Petta
Finish	Cala Gonone
Total ascent	250m (820ft)
Total descent	1150m (3775ft)
Time	8hrs
Map	IGMI 'Serie 50' 500 and 517, 'Serie 25' 500 II and 517 I
Terrain	A track and rugged paths descend into the valley. A riverside path gives way to a rugged riverbed. A popular coast path and road are used at the end.
Refreshment	Bar at Cala Luna; plenty of choice in Cala Gonone
Transport/access	Infrequent daily buses serve Genna 'e Petta from Dorgali and Tortolí; regular daily buses serve Cala Gonone from Dorgali and Nuoro. An optional boat pick-up can be arranged at Cala Luna, but do this well in advance, in person, by making enquiries at the harbour in Cala Gonone.
Note	Descent uses waymarked trail 181

View from Genna 'e Petta, beyond the forestry house, across the deep-cut Codula Luna

Most visitors to the deep-cleft Codula Luna explore only part of the valley, from Teletotes or Cala Luna, because they have to return to their cars. Few realise that a linear walk is possible, with bus access at Genna 'e Petta and Cala Gonone, and the option to arrange a boat pick-up at Cala Luna.

Genna 'e Petta is a gap at Km187 on the bleak mountain road high above Su Gorropu, at 900m (2950ft). There are two gates beside the road – one for Sa Portiscra (Walk 10), and the other for today's walk, signposted 'Cala Luna' and flashed red/white. Follow the track down from the roadside gate, through another gate, round a valley, then note a pinnettu on the left at **Gosollei**. When a **forestry house**

is reached, turn left along a track winding down a wooded slope. Stay on the main track, avoid a lesser track on the right, but turn right at a signposted junction by a tiny stone hut. Turn right at

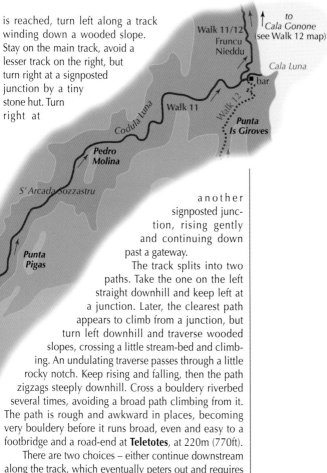

another signposted junction, rising gently and continuing down past a gateway.

The track splits into two paths. Take the one on the left straight downhill and keep left at a junction. Later, the clearest path appears to climb from a junction, but turn left downhill and traverse wooded slopes, crossing a little stream-bed and climbing. An undulating traverse passes through a little rocky notch. Keep rising and falling, then the path zigzags steeply downhill. Cross a bouldery riverbed several times, avoiding a broad path climbing from it. The path is rough and awkward in places, becoming very bouldery before it runs broad, even and easy to a footbridge and a road-end at **Teletotes**, at 220m (770ft).

There are two choices – either continue downstream along the track, which eventually peters out and requires the river to be forded, or cross the footbridge and follow a narrow path downstream, without the need to ford the river. Both options are signposted, but there are no more signposts along the length of **Codula Luna**. Whatever choice is made, follow the path on the eastern bank later, which crosses a metal ladder-stile.

Follow the path faithfully. Sometimes it peters out beside the river, but look for its continuation, rather than boulder-hop along the riverbed. The path climbs high for a while, and some lower parts are clogged by driftwood. The woods may be brambly, but the path can be covered more quickly than the riverbed. Later, the path expires completely and the riverbed must be followed. If there is water flowing then it may be necessary to ford. There are swallow-holes later and it is rare to find water beyond them. Boulder-hop, crunch across shoals of gravel, cross soft sandbanks and avoid tangled oleasters in the riverbed.

The valley sides are steep and rocky, and there are pronounced bends in the riverbed. When a broad and sandy stretch is reached, it is possible to exit left and follow a level path through bushy and grassy areas, but if this can't be located continue along the riverbed until a stone-built block is noticed on the left. A path leaves the valley here for Cala Gonone, and anyone in a hurry will follow it straight away (see Walk 12 for a route description). Others may choose to visit the **bar/restaurant** on the right or the nearby beach at **Cala Luna** before retracing their steps and continuing the 8km (5 miles) to **Cala Gonone**. ◄

Arranging a boat pick-up here saves walking to Cala Gonone.

WALK 12
Cala Sisine, Cala Luna and Cala Gonone

Distance	25km (15½ miles)
Start	Codula Sisine
Finish	Cala Gonone
Total ascent	950m (315ft)
Total descent	1100m (3610ft)
Time	8hrs
Map	IGMI 'Serie 50' 500 and 517, 'Serie 25' 500 II and 517 I

Terrain	Good valley track at first, then rough and stony paths uphill and downhill, sometimes near the coast, ending with a road-walk
Refreshment	Bars at Cala Sisine and Cala Luna; plenty of choice in Cala Gonone
Transport/access	No public transport between Baunei and Golgo. Pick-ups and drop-offs by boat can be arranged at Cala Sisine and Cala Luna, but do this well in advance, in person, by making enquiries at the harbour in Cala Gonone. Regular daily buses serve Cala Gonone from Dorgali and Nuoro.
Note	To reach the start, arrange a lift from Baunei to the Golgo plateau, then drive along a dirt road marked 'Cala Sisine'. If your driver baulks at the end of the tarmacked road at San Pietro, it's a walk of 10km (6 miles) along the dirt road to Codula Sisine.

Most walkers visiting Cala Sisine and Cala Luna end up retracing their steps. To avoid there-and-back walks to these remote beaches, arrange a lift to the start at Codula Sisine. Walk down to the valley to Cala Sisine, over to Cala Luna, and finish at Cala Gonone.

Walk off the end of the stone-paved road at **Codula Sisine**, at 150m (490ft). Turn right and cross the riverbed, then cross it again and again. On the way down through the valley, a couple of tracks will be seen climbing to the left, but stay low, crossing and recrossing the riverbed repeatedly. Sometimes the slopes are wooded, and at other times the riverbed is flanked by sheer and even overhanging cliffs. A barrier finally prevents motorists continuing any further.

Map continues on page 72

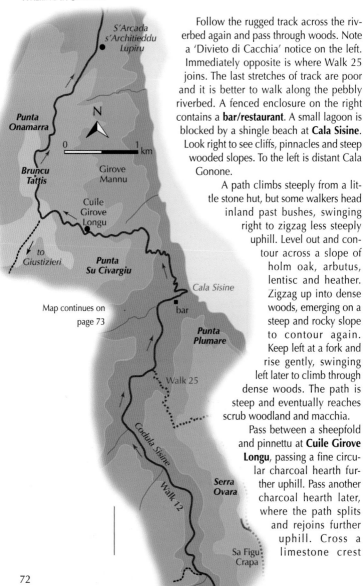

Follow the rugged track across the riverbed again and pass through woods. Note a 'Divieto di Cacchia' notice on the left. Immediately opposite is where Walk 25 joins. The last stretches of track are poor and it is better to walk along the pebbly riverbed. A fenced enclosure on the right contains a **bar/restaurant**. A small lagoon is blocked by a shingle beach at **Cala Sisine**. Look right to see cliffs, pinnacles and steep wooded slopes. To the left is distant Cala Gonone.

A path climbs steeply from a little stone hut, but some walkers head inland past bushes, swinging right to zigzag less steeply uphill. Level out and contour across a slope of holm oak, arbutus, lentisc and heather. Zigzag up into dense woods, emerging on a steep and rocky slope to contour again. Keep left at a fork and rise gently, swinging left later to climb through dense woods. The path is steep and eventually reaches scrub woodland and macchia.

Pass between a sheepfold and pinnettu at **Cuile Girove Longu**, passing a fine circular charcoal hearth further uphill. Pass another charcoal hearth later, where the path splits and rejoins further uphill. Cross a limestone crest around 650m (2130ft), walk down to a track and turn right to follow it, undulating and winding, with occasional views of Cala Gonone. Bushes are dotted across the rocky slopes and the tallest trees are junipers. Pass more charcoal hearths and spot 'Cala Luna' carved on rocks a few times. The track descends among dense juniper, holm oak, arbutus and heather. Watch on the right to spot a prominent rock window – **S'Arcada s'Architieddu Lupiru** – which is worth a short detour.

Map continues on page 74

The broad path runs down through the valley, passing bushy euphorbia. Zigzag uphill on basalt as well as limestone, cross a crest, then zigzag down a rough and stony path. Turn right at a **bar/restaurant** at the bottom, or turn left to head straight for Cala Gonone. The path reaches a lagoon, and if water stretches from cliff to cliff it is necessary to wade across to the beach at **Cala Luna**. Head back past the bar/restaurant, through a gate and across a broad and sandy riverbed. ▸

A stone-built block marks a path running level through woods. Follow it and watch for a right turn up a rock-step, then climb a rugged path through dense woods. Cross a basalt bed while turning a corner, enjoying a view back to Cala Luna. The gradient eases, but the path is bouldery. Watch for a right turn down awkward, lumpy limestone. Later, watch for another right turn downhill. Climb steeply up a rocky ramp and pass the mouth of a cave, **Grotta Oddoanna**.

Pick a way across a rocky slope and the path becomes easier underfoot, winding and undulating through woods. Climb a little, head gently downhill, then go down steep, rugged

Sos
Furones

Cala Fuili

Grotta del
Bue Marino

Walk 11
joins here.

**Puntale
Mannu**

Grotta
Oddoanna

Walk 12
Fruncu
Nieddu

Cala Luna

Bar

Walk 11

**Punta
Is Giroves**

S'Arcada
s'Architieddu
Lupiru

73

Looking along the cliff coastline from Cala Luna towards Cala Gonone

zigzags into a rock-walled canyon, where there is access to a pebbly beach at **Cala Fuili**. If you are not visiting the beach, climb a fenced, zigzagged path to a road-end, then simply follow the road for 3km (2 miles) to **Cala Gonone**. Buses turn a corner near the Km1 marker; otherwise, walk straight into town and enjoy its full range of services.

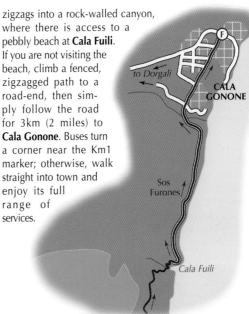

74

WALK 13
Giustizieri and Sa Coronas

Distance	13km (via short-cut) or 19km (8 or 12 miles)
Start/finish	Casa Cantoniera, Giustizieri
Total ascent/descent	250 or 500m (820 or 1640ft)
Time	3hrs 30min or 5hrs
Map	IGMI 'Serie 50' 517, 'Serie 25' 517 I and II
Terrain	Gentle and obvious tracks rise and fall on slopes of macchia
Refreshment	None
Transport/access	Infrequent daily buses serve Giustizieri from Dorgali, Urzulei and Tortolí

Giustizieri is at a high and remote road junction, in an area of granite surrounded by rugged limestone mountains, criss-crossed by a network of easy tracks. Although there is plenty of dense macchia, woodland and bare rock, large areas are grazed by cattle, sheep, goats and pigs and the 'Goroppu' cheese-making farm can be visited towards the end of the walk. There is an optional short-cut that reduces the walk by 6km.

Start at the main road junction near the crumbling Casa Cantoniera (road-worker's house) at 738m (2421ft) at **Giustizieri**. A broad dirt road runs gently downhill past areas of rough grazing and patchy macchia, all on granite bedrock. Climb gently up and around a corner, crossing slopes of arbutus and heather. Tall alder trees grow beside small streams on the way round a valley, passing a goat farm. Climb gently up and around the slope, levelling out. When a **junction** is reached, keep right downhill for the full route, or go left for an easier short-cut that rejoins the main route before Genna Croce. (Stay on the clearest track to take the short-cut route, and avoid a right turn to Cuile Olelai.)

For the full route, follow the track downhill, avoiding all lesser tracks branching from it, wind down through scrub woodland and eventually cross a bouldery stream-bed, where there might be a waterfall. There are some tall holm oaks around here, and plenty of cistus beside the track. Walk round into a valley and cross a bouldery stream, below 700m (2300ft), climbing the other side past tall holm oaks. Take the line of least resistance at **Oddai** through dense cistus, passing arbutus, heather and a small stand of alder.

The track climbs rough and stony from **Bruncu Stasighe**, with a bendy stretch alongside a fence. Keep climbing as views expand, crossing a slight dip, levelling out, then making a gentle ascent across a slope of arbutus and heather at **Sa Coronas**, around 800m (2625ft). The path overlooks a grazed area surrounded by mountains. Cross half a dozen stream-beds as the track eventually turns directly southwards, still on granite, but at the foot of a range of limestone mountains far below a road. Another track comes down on the right, but keep straight

Map labels: Bruncu E Surgano; to Dorgali; tunnels; Sa Coronas; Bruncu Stasighe; Cuile Olelai; Oddai; N; 0 1 km; 900m Genna Croce; goat farm; Serra Tranapia; Walk 14; farm; Walk 13; 738m Giustizieri; to Baunei; SF

ahead, generally ascending gently. (A clear dirt road joins on the left, used by the short-cut route from Cuile Olelai.)

Keep climbing straight ahead, past rough grazing and scrub woodland, towards tall holm oak and arbutus on limestone slopes. The ascent leads to the main road at **Genna Croce**, around 900m (2950ft), near a curious building, the Gorropu trekking centre. ▶ Turn left to walk down the bendy road, taking great care at weekends, when motorcyclists may be out in force, and at great speed. There is only one short-cut through the road bends, as well as access to a farm where Gorropu cheese is sold. If you stop to buy cheese, there is a short-cut over a ladder-stile onto the road, leading quickly back to the road junction at **Giustizieri**.

A stony track flanked by polka-dot cistus leads between the hills near Sa Coronas

Walk 14 ends here.

WALK 14
Genna Silana to Genna Croce

Distance	11km (7 miles)
Start	Genna Silana
Finish	Genna Croce
Total ascent	635m (2085ft)
Total descent	740m (2430ft)
Time	6hrs
Map	IGMI 'Serie 50' 517, 'Serie 25' 517 I
Terrain	Rocky and pathless, needing care throughout, with some hands-on scrambling
Refreshment	Bar at Genna Silana
Transport/access	Infrequent daily buses serve Genna Silana and Genna Croce from Dorgali and Tortolí

The mountain road between Genna Silana and Genna Croce has steep slopes and sheer cliffs above it. A rocky ridge studded with peaks runs north–south, rugged and pathless, but walkable with due care and attention, and this offers a splendid traverse for tough and sure-footed walkers.

Start at **Genna Silana**, 1017m (3337ft), where a roadside signpost indicates 'Punta Cucuttos'. Walk down a stony track and almost immediately fork left down a path, then spot vague wheel-marks climbing to a tall holm oak tree. Turn left to climb a steep, stony, rocky slope, where the macchia is grazed low by goats. Look ahead to spot the best line past stout holm oaks and junipers. It drifts onto easy-angled rock and scree, then reaches the crest of Costa Silana, around 1200m (3940ft).

Turn left, following the crest southwards past juniper bushes, limestone outcrops and stony patches. Cross a gentle gap and allow the geography, geology and scanty goat paths to work together. There is a fine view back

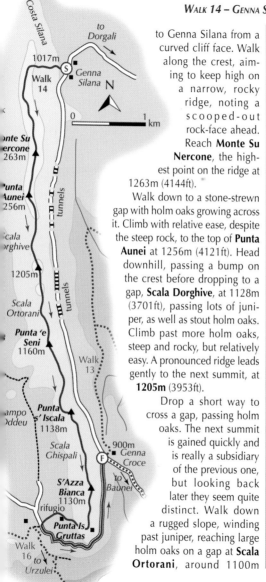

to Genna Silana from a curved cliff face. Walk along the crest, aiming to keep high on a narrow, rocky ridge, noting a scooped-out rock-face ahead. Reach **Monte Su Nercone**, the highest point on the ridge at 1263m (4144ft).

Walk down to a stone-strewn gap with holm oaks growing across it. Climb with relative ease, despite the steep rock, to the top of **Punta Aunei** at 1256m (4121ft). Head downhill, passing a bump on the crest before dropping to a gap, **Scala Dorghive**, at 1128m (3701ft), passing lots of juniper, as well as stout holm oaks. Climb past more holm oaks, steep and rocky, but relatively easy. A pronounced ridge leads gently to the next summit, at **1205m** (3953ft).

Drop a short way to cross a gap, passing holm oaks. The next summit is gained quickly and is really a subsidiary of the previous one, but looking back later they seem quite distinct. Walk down a rugged slope, winding past juniper, reaching large holm oaks on a gap at **Scala Ortorani**, around 1100m

79

(3610ft). Climb to the next summit, which is indistinct, but note the tilted limestone pavement as juniper thins out, and a big semi-circular bite out of the pavement later.

Walk on tilted slabs onto the bare-slab summit of **Punta 'e Seni**, at 1160m (3806ft). Walk downhill, first on slabs, then winding past juniper over a subsidiary summit. Continue down, looking back to see how the subsidiary looks splendid in its own right. The next gap, around 1050m (3445ft), is broad and distinctive, with a drystone wall separating holm oaks from juniper. Ahead is a prominent conical peak, but its shape changes to a monstrous, overhanging dome.

Climb directly from a big holm oak, passing sparse juniper, and pick the easiest-looking line while scrambling up limestone slabs. **Punta s'Iscala** rises to 1138m (3734ft), with two rocky tops separated by a dramatic cleft. Walk down past a holm oak, picking a way down rocky ribs past juniper, reaching a gap at **Scala Ghispali**, around 1050m (3445ft). There is a view left down to Genna Croce – the end of the walk – but still a long way away!

The final part of the ridge, beyond S'Azza Bianca, involves plenty of hands-on scrambling

Climb steep and rugged, crossing a wire fence on the crest, to reach a metal pole on top of **S'Azza Bianca**, at 1130m (3707ft). Scramble along and down a sinuous rocky crest, which is narrow, steep-sided, split by clefts and rather daunting in places. Keep scrambling towards

a final little peak. The crest remains rough and rocky, but is covered in juniper bushes, so weave between them to reach a hut on **Punta Is Gruttas**, overlooking a fine valley.

Swing right to pick up a fine track, but leave it to drop down steep rock and stony patches, picking up the access track from the **Rifugio Lampattu** to a road. ▶ Turn left to follow the road away from the level **Campu Oddeu**, slicing across an impressive cliff high above Urzulei. The road rises gently to a junction at **Genna Croce**, around 900m (2950ft), near the Gorropu trekking centre. ▶

Walk 16 can be joined here to descend to Urzulei.

Walk 13 joins here.

WALK 15
Coile Orbisi and Sa Pischina

Distance	15km (9½ miles)
Start/finish	Near Codula Orbisi
Total ascent/descent	300m (985ft)
Time	5hrs
Map	IGMI 'Serie 50' 517, 'Serie 25' 517 IV
Terrain	Good woodland tracks at the start and finish, with rugged paths and rocky slopes in the middle
Refreshment	None
Transport/access	The start is 6km (4 miles) from a bus route at Genna Croce. Cars can be driven from Genna Croce onto Campo Oddeu, where tarmac gives way to a dirt road signposted as a walking trail and flashed red/white.
Note	Route uses waymarked trail 502

Visitors to Gola de Su Gorropu (Walk 7) often wonder what lies further up the gorge, but are unable to scale it. This walk forges towards Gorropu from the top, though it stops well short of the gorge, and explores the rugged Codula Orbisi that feeds into it. After visiting a huge, water-filled hole at Sa Pischina, an easy track is used to return to the starting point.

Start at a junction where the trail is signposted off the dirt road, around 925m (3035ft), before **Codula Orbisi**. Follow a track on the right, signposted 'Sedda ar Baccas' and 'Gorropu'. ◄ Rugged, rolling limestone is dotted with juniper bushes, and the track passes a few big holm oak trees, undulating gently. When another junction is reached, keep left downhill among holm oaks, spotting a **sheepfold**. Keep straight ahead, rising and falling gently. Views between the trees take in a gorge and distant mountains. A path marked by small cairns heads right, but stay on the stony track leading downhill. The track appears to rise later, but this is actually a stony line enclosed by limestone outcrops. Watch instead for a vague cairned path to the left among dense holm oaks, showing signs of vehicular use.

Note that the route returns along the dirt road.

The path climbs gradually past a small, tumbled **pinnettu**, and becomes vague and rugged as it climbs beside a rock rib. It levels out and later runs downhill, marked by cairns and flanked by stones. Stay on it across bare rock and stony slopes, and through patchy holm oak woods. Emerge into a sloping clearing where there is a gnarled, fallen tree. A sheepfold lies straight downhill, but don't go there – instead find a cairned path marked by lines of stones, winding down to a pinnettu and sheepfold at **Coile Orbisi**, at 811m (2661ft).

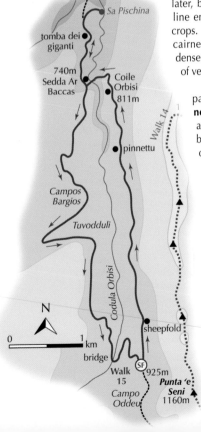

82

Looking into the deep, dark, water-filled rocky gorge at Sa Pischina

Keep right of this site to follow the cairned path further downhill. There is a sudden view of the limestone gorge of Codula Orbisi, with a prominent pinnettu on the far side. Go down the path, either walking on stones as marked by cairns or down a slab of bare limestone. Either way, land in the bed of the gorge between rock walls. Turn left, but watch for a path climbing on the right, cairned and mostly on sloping rock. At the top, the gates of the farm **Sedda Ar Baccas** are reached at 740m (2430ft).

Turn right and follow a track down among holm oaks, passing an enormous yew, then rising through an open

The track runs to the
Riu Flumineddu,
above Gola de
Su Gorropu, but
anyone going down
must climb back
afterwards.

space where a tumbled **tomba dei giganti** (burial chamber) is located. Follow the track further downhill. ◀ A path is signposted down a steep and loose slope to **Sa Pischina**, which is an amazing sight. A big water hole is surrounded on most sides by overhanging rock, while the riverbed is a mass of huge boulders. Retrace steps back to **Sedda Ar Baccas**.

The track is stone-paved for a while as it climbs from the farmstead, then it runs stony and obvious, generally rising through woods. There is an open space at **Campos Bargios**, around 850m (2790ft). The track climbs and turns sharp left, later overlooking the valley. Descend gently, with one stretch being stone-paved, and continue down through woods. After another stone-paved descent the track swings left, crosses a bridge over **Codula Orbisi**, and bends as it climbs back to the junction where the walk started on the edge of **Campo Oddeu**.

WALK 16
Fennau, Televai and Urzulei

Distance	9km (to Fennau) or 17km (to Urzulei) (5½ or 10½ miles)
Start/finish	Fennau
Alternative finish	Urzulei
Total ascent	200 or 450m (650 or 1475ft)
Total descent	200m or 850m (650 or 2790ft)
Time	2hrs 30min or 5hrs
Map	IGMI 'Serie 50' 517, 'Serie 25' 517 I, II, III and IV
Terrain	Easy roads and tracks at first, but rugged paths and a steep, wooded descent at the end
Refreshment	Bars at Urzulei
Transport/access	Televai is 5km (3 miles) from a bus route at Genna Croce. Cars can be driven from Genna Croce to Televai and Fennau. There is a lay-by before the tarmac ends at Fennau, around 975m (3200ft).
Note	Route mostly uses waymarked trail 501

A well-engineered path crosses a rocky slope above the river on the way to Televai

The main route is a circuit from Fennau via Televai, although on returning to Fennau the route can be extended to run over the mountains and then descend to Urzulei. The choice depends on whether you need to return to a car, or whether you can arrange appropriate drop-offs and pick-ups.

At **Fennau**, a signposted walking trail crosses the road. This trail, Sentiero San Giorgio, is numbered 501 and flashed red/white. Pigs usually forage near the lay-by, and before the walk is finished expect to see cattle, goats, sheep, donkeys, horses and dogs too. Walk down a track signposted for 'Lecceta Primaria', cross a river-bed and climb past stout holm oaks. There is no path and it is often rocky underfoot, but a vague vehicle track should be spotted down the other side. Trees thin out and a broad riverbed is crossed. Aim for a track junction beside a water trough at **Su Feu**, at 940m (3085ft). The

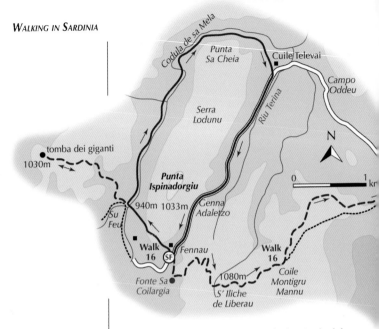

main circuit turns right here, alongside the riverbed, but the other track offers an interesting extension.

Extension to tomba dei giganti (4km/2½ miles return)
Follow the track signposted 'Tomba dei giganti', winding up well-grazed slopes dotted with trees and avoiding other tracks to end at 1030m (3380ft). There are two burial chambers (tomba dei giganti) just to the left. The passages are neatly constructed, flanked by curved walls, and overlook a limestone edge with fine view of the mountains. Retrace your steps back down to Su Feu.

Follow a clear track alongside the riverbed, past a pig pen and onwards to a couple of water troughs. Continue along a vague animal path parallel to the river. Cross the riverbed at a sandbank and pass a small area of macchia. Cross the riverbed at a pebbly stretch and follow a vague path onwards. Cross the riverbed a third time where limestone is exposed and pick up a clear path climbing gently. It has a built-up edge and crosses a steep, rugged slope dotted with holm oaks. Turn a rocky corner overlooking the gorge of **Codula de sa Mela**. Outcrops lean over the path, and there are splendid views each time a rocky corner is turned. Descend among patchy holm oaks and pass a farm at **Cuile Televai** to reach a road around 900m (2950ft).

Turn right to follow the road gently uphill, cut into schist bedrock, with the **Riu Terina** flowing parallel. Cross a bridge and climb more steeply, with juniper, heather and broom alongside, and arbutus further uphill. Cross a gentle gap, **Genna Adaletzo**, at 1033m (3389ft). The road returns to the lay-by where this circuit started. Either finish here or turn left as signposted to 'Urzulei'.

Extension to Urzulei (8km/5 miles)

To continue to Urzulei, climb a pathless, grassy slope, drifting right to follow a grassy track through dense macchia. Cross a little stream-bed, with the route rising and falling to a picnic site at **Fonte Sa Coilargia**. Turn left up a track which soon terminates. Keep well left of a stream-bed, climbing and zigzagging onto a less bushy crest. Climb straight uphill, over a rounded crest, passing two small upright stones. Follow a path downhill, undulating past heather and occasional juniper and crossing a couple of little stream-beds, followed by a short, steep descent to a bigger stream among stout holm oaks.

Climb past a signpost at **S' Iliche de Liberau**, at 1080m (3545ft), leaving the oaks for more heather and juniper. A level and easy stretch passes right of a rocky knoll, then the path is steep and rugged down into a valley full of holm oaks. Pass a hut at **Coile Montigru Mannu**, at 1070m (3510ft), and continue down to cross a stream. Climb a short, steep, rugged path and cross a little stream-bed. Watch for a small animal pen on the left and spot a path climbing to the right of it. (There is a more obvious track, but do not follow it.)

The path crosses a slope of heather, juniper and holm oak scrub, drops gently to cross a stream-bed, then rises to cross a track. Walk towards a rocky summit that has been cleft in two. Stone uprights mark a route below rock buttresses on a slope of big limestone boulders. The path is vague beyond, but joins a track at a signpost. Turn left down to a gap, with views across the plain of **Campu Oddeu** and down a broad valley. A solitary farm lies to the left, and a signpost points right for Urzulei.

Walk down through a little valley among holm oaks. Watch carefully for a buttressed path to the left, zigzagging downhill. Cross a trodden fence and continue down to a track. However, turn right to leave it, following a vague path among pines and joining a winding track. There is a view of **Urzulei** before the first houses and a signpost are reached. Either short-cut left down stone steps or turn right up a concrete road, rising and falling along a panoramic tarmac road, Via Della Pineta. Follow a dirt road onwards and turn left down Via San Sebastiano to the chapel of San Giorgio on the main road. (There are bars and a shop, if food and drink are needed while waiting for a bus.)

WALK 17
Talana and Nuraghe Bau e Tanca

Distance	11km (7 miles)
Start/finish	Church in Talana
Total ascent	550m (1805ft)
Total descent	550m (1805ft)
Time	4hrs
Map	IGMI 'Serie 50' 517, 'Serie 25' 517 IV
Terrain	Roads, forest tracks and a few rugged paths
Refreshment	Bars in Talana
Transport/access	Regular daily buses serve Talana from Lotzoraì and Urzulei

Talana clings to a steep and well-wooded mountainside, and the woodpiles standing alongside houses suggest that it could be chilly in the winter months. Above the woods lies a broad and level gap where a nuraghic settlement with a well-preserved tower can be studied, close to the route at Nuraghe Bau e Tanca.

Start at the church in **Talana**, around 650m (2130ft), and follow the road into the village to reach a signposted road junction. Turn right, as signposted for 'schools' and 'Funtana e Figili', along the Via Regina Elena. Fork left up Via Alessandro Manzoni, and either follow this bendy road to the Scuola Materna or short-cut up flights of concrete steps to reach the school. Either way, continue along the road as signposted for 'Funtana e Figili'. The road bends left, right and left again.

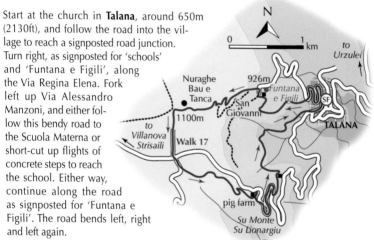

At the next bend, turn left along a track, passing a water building and rising past holm oaks and arbutus. Cross a stream-bed, climbing and undulating, passing through gates, then descend and cross another stream-bed. Pass a concrete hut, turn sharp right at a junction and climb, reaching the derelict modern chapel of **San Giovanni** at 926m (3038ft). Turn left up to a road, turn right down the road, then left up a track. ▸

The track climbs through holm oak woods with some arbutus and heather. Keep left at a junction, pass a fence, then climb a boulder-paved path, clear and obvious, across a granite cliff. Scramble a short way to a bouldery stream-bed and turn left along a clear track to

To visit the nearby spring of Funtana e Figili, go further down the road, then return to this point.

An old path, hacked into a well-wooded, granite slope, reaches a broad and gentle upland plain

continue uphill. This finally leaves the woods and passes a fence on a high crest, then leads onto a plateau of juniper and heather bushes, with asphodel, bracken and fragrant scrub, grazed by sheep and goats. Follow the track very gently downhill until **Nuraghe Bau e Tanca**, around 1100m (3610ft), can be reached on the right. Inspect it carefully, noting its double walls, spiral staircase and surrounding hut foundations.

Follow the track onwards and turn left. The track becomes a road leading to a crossroads. Cross the road as if intending to climb Monte Olinie. Walk up the road a little and turn left, heading gently up a track across a grassy slope. Pass a few junipers, level out, then head downhill along a rougher and stonier track flanked by bracken, heather and broom. Wind down past a goat and **pig farm**, then down through woods to the road, landing on a bend. Turn right down the road, then left and right round bends on the slopes of **Su Monte Su Lionargiu**.

Watch for a sharp left turn down a clear track across a wooded slope. Another track comes down steeply from the left. Pass a property shielded by a fence and reach its gate. The track forks, so keep left, round a left bend, still heading downhill. Walk round a valley full of tall trees, down through gates and past small cultivated areas overlooking Talana. Continue down and round the slope to cross two bridges close together. The track is gentle as it heads directly towards **Talana**, becoming concrete at the first building. Walk straight onwards and follow the main road into the village centre. Shops and bars offer food and drink, and there are bus services.

WALK 18
Monte Olinie to Coe Serra

Distance	13km (8 miles)
Start	Monte Olinie
Finish	Coe Serra
Total ascent	130m (425ft)
Total descent	1350m (4430ft)
Time	4hrs
Map	IGMI 'Serie 50' 517, 'Serie 25' 517 III and 517 II
Terrain	Mostly downhill on good tracks and paths, on slopes of scrub and forest
Refreshment	None
Transport/access	No public transport to the summit of Monte Olinie. Regular daily buses link Coe Serra with Talana, Lotzoraì and Urzulei. This route works only if a drop-off can be arranged on Monte Olinie, although strong walkers could climb Monte Olinie from Talana by following Walk 17, then going up the mountain road and track, and then descending. The last 3km (2 miles) to the summit is a driveable track.
Note	Route uses waymarked trail 531

Monte Olinie is a notable viewpoint whose summit bears a lookout tower that can be reached by car. From there a fine route runs down scrub and forested slopes, featuring a remarkable restored stone stairway at one point. The walk finishes deep in the valley at Coe Serra, from where it can be linked with other routes, notably Walk 20.

to Villanova Strisaili

pig farm

to Talana

Su Monte Su Lionargiu

Bruncu Tortari

Riu Mortor

Toccedorgo

agriturismo

Riu Figarba

Riu Sa Minzo

S'atza 'e Mesu

road broken

Sorberine

575m

forestry house

1372m Monte Olinie (S)

Walk 18

N

Chirriddiu Sa Caffa der Beccoso

Serra 'e Monte

to Villanova Strisaili

0   1 km

Monte Olinie is crowned with a prominent fire lookout tower at 1372m (4501ft), along with a mapboard and a signpost for the Sentiero Sorberine. Enjoy views

Following a clear path down the bushy, wooded slopes of Monte Olinie

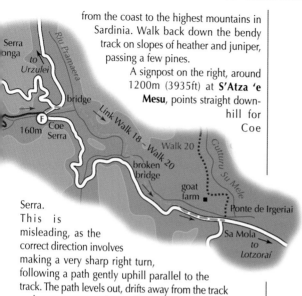

from the coast to the highest mountains in Sardinia. Walk back down the bendy track on slopes of heather and juniper, passing a few pines.

A signpost on the right, around 1200m (3935ft) at **S'Atza 'e Mesu**, points straight downhill for Coe Serra. This is misleading, as the correct direction involves making a very sharp right turn, following a path gently uphill parallel to the track. The path levels out, drifts away from the track and crosses a steep slope of heather. Zigzag down a blunt ridge, rocky in places, with views north to Talana. The path drops into denser bushes and mixed forest, with fewer views. Cross a bouldery stream-bed and follow a broader path on a falling traverse. However, watch for a signpost and a narrower path down to the right.

Reach a road at **Serra 'e Monte**, around 750m (2460ft). ▶ Cross the road and pick up the path as signposted – it is level at first, then goes gently down to a junction. A short spur on the right leads to the rocky **Chirriddiu Sa Caffa der Beccoso**, but turn left to stay on the route. The path drops steep, rugged and narrow, crosses a stream-bed and climbs to reach a track. Turn right down the track and go through gates to reach a picnic site at a forestry house (*casermetta forestale*) on a gap around 575m (1885ft) at **Sorberine**.

Keep right of the furthest building and go through a gap in a fence to continue along the path, making a rising traverse across a forested slope. Reach a signpost

Traffic cannot use this road to link Talana and Villagrande Strisaili because of a nearby landslide.

and keep left to stay on the route. Walk down to another path junction at **Toccedorgo**, at 425m (1395ft), and keep straight ahead, climbing gently.

Fenced flights of stone steps climb uphill a short way, then zigzag downhill. A series of fenced, winding stone stairways drop down a rocky slope, all wonderfully restored. Keep right of a small goat farm and walk down its access track. This leads across a concrete culvert in the broad, rubble-strewn bed of **Riu Mortorinci**. Walk up to a mapboard and turn right to follow a track down to a road bend and bridge at **Coe Serra**, at 160m (525ft). Keep left along the road to reach a junction where buses can be caught.

Restored stone steps take the path down a ridge towards Coe Serra

Link with Walk 20 (3km/2 miles)

Just along the road from Coe Serra, a signpost indicates the Sentiero dei Carbonai trail. Follow a track drifting away from the road, through woodland, to a crumbling stone bridge spanning the Riu Pramaera. Cross over and turn right, following a rugged track downstream. This was a highway in its time, but is little more than a path today. Another old stone bridge is reached, but only one arch remains and the river is sometimes impassable. If the river can be crossed, then continue downstream until forced onto the road. (If the river cannot be crossed then it is possible, but awkward, to continue downstream.) Walk along the road and turn left to cross a stout concrete bridge, Ponte de Irgeriai, at 100m (330ft), to follow Walk 20.

WALK 19

Talana and Coe Serra

Distance	16km (10 miles)
Start/finish	Church in Talana
Total ascent/descent	550m (1805ft)
Time	6hrs
Map	IGMI 'Serie 50' 517, 'Serie 25' II and III
Terrain	Paths through macchia, tracks through forest, rugged riverbeds and roads
Refreshment	Bars in Talana
Transport/access	Regular daily buses serve Talana and Coe Serra from Lotzoraì and Urzule

Talana clings to a wooded mountainside, and this walk heads down into a valley, then climbs back to the village. A bus route divides the walk, so it can be split into two unequal sections. Note that the descent cannot be attempted if the river running through the valley is in flood.

Start at the church in **Talana**, around 650m (2130ft), and walk between it and a nearby bar, down the newly stone-paved Via Santa Maria Maddalena. When a complex road junction is reached, follow the only road rising gently, passing a school on the broader Piazza Santa Maria Maddalena. Step down a concrete ramp on the right to pick up a narrow path between brambles. It appears only to serve small cultivated patches, but actually crosses little stream-beds and heads away from the village. It is cut through schist and flanked by rich macchia, and trees, notably holm oaks. There is a good view back to Talana from a corner.

Follow the path gently down between old terraces and cross a stream-bed. Crude rock-steps lead uphill and round a corner as the trees thin out and the

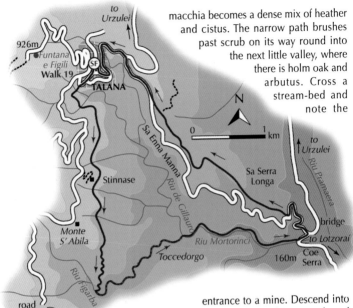

macchia becomes a dense mix of heather and cistus. The narrow path brushes past scrub on its way round into the next little valley, where there is holm oak and arbutus. Cross a stream-bed and note the

entrance to a mine. Descend into the next wooded valley, making an awkward crossing of a stream-bed, then climb schist rock-steps and pass a fenced enclosure around a small farm at **Stinnase**.

Turn right up an access track and left to pick up a clear, stony track running above other small farm buildings and enclosures. This runs gently down across a wooded slope overlooking conifer plantations. Follow the track to a bend overlooking a valley, turn left down a worn, stony path, then right at a junction down a stony path past cistus and heather. Cross a stream-bed and climb a more wooded slope on the flank of **Monte S'Abila**. Fork left at a junction, down into the conifers, where the ground scrub is dense and varied. The path appears to drop into a deep and rugged valley, but swings left to avoid it. Later, bend right and drop more steeply in dense forest, and take care to follow the path even when trees are growing on top of it. There is a final left bend and a short rock-step down to the bed of **Riu Figarba**, which features massive heaps of sand, gravel, pebbles and boulders. Broken, scoured tree trunks tell of this river's power when in full flood.

Turn left to walk downstream, and the riverbed narrows dramatically, with walls of schist and pink granite. Take care passing log jams, watch where feet are being placed, and enjoy the confines of the gorge. When the riverbed broadens again, watch for stretches of an old track on either side. When a rock bar is reached, the old track crosses from right to left and should be followed to avoid a gorge further downstream. There is later a longer stretch of track on the left bank, leading to a

stone ruin at a confluence with the **Riu de Gillauro**. Cross this river and continue downstream on the left bank of the **Riu Mortorinci**, but watch as the track switches sides over and over again. A mapboard is seen where Walk 18 joins, so walk straight ahead and follow the track down to a road bend and bridge at **Coe Serra**, at 160m (525ft).

Water levels in the Riu Figarba must be low enough to allow walkers through the valley

Keep left along the road to reach a junction where buses can be caught, or turn left to climb back to Talana. To do this, pass the kilometre marker signs, first Km15, then up the bendy road to Km16. Immediately after this, scramble up the rocky roadside cutting onto dense macchia above. Aim to follow the crest at first, but watch carefully to pick up and follow a vague trodden line over a hump ahead, then keep right of a rocky hump. Stay on the crest of **Sa Serra Longa**, and a grassy track is joined quite suddenly.

Follow the track to a junction and keep left along a stony track. This runs up across a slope of arbutus, heather and holm oaks, turning right round a bend overlooking the slope of **Sa Enna Manna**, with Talana seen ahead. Go through a gateway in a fence, down and uphill, through another gateway in a fence and across a slope of scrub woodland to reach a junction. Keep left and walk gently down to the road. Turn right to walk up the road, passing a junction and a wayside shrine. Keep left and walk round a wooded valley, passing a cemetery to finish back at the church in **Talana**. (There are bars and shops, if there is time while waiting for a bus.)

WALK 20
Sa Mola and Paule Munduge

Distance	10km or (with extension to Predu Orrubiu) 15km (6 or 9½ miles)
Start/finish	Ponte de Irgeriai, Sa Mola
Total ascent/descent	600m (1970ft)
Time	3hrs 30min or 5hrs
Map	IGMI 'Serie 50' 517, 'Serie 25' 517 II
Terrain	Easy tracks and rugged paths, steep at times, on wooded and rocky slopes
Refreshment	None
Transport/access	Regular daily buses link Sa Mola with Talana, Lotzoraì and Urzulei. As the bus approaches on the road from Lotzoraì, watch for the Km10 marker at Sa Mola, then for the stout concrete bridge of Ponte de Irgeriai.
Note	Route uses waymarked trail 532

This walk explores a former charcoal-burning area, where workers lived on the job in simple *dispensa* buildings. Woodlands cling to steep and rocky slopes. In winter and spring there should be a shallow pool at Paule Munduge, although this usually dries completely in the summer. The longer version of the walk follows an easy route with views and visits a ruin at Predu Orrubiu.

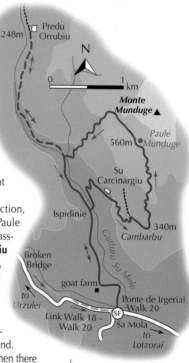

Beyond the Km10 marker at **Sa Mola** continue along the road to the bridge of **Ponte de Irgeriai**, at 100m (330ft). A signpost lists several destinations along the Sentiero dei Carbonai. Follow a dirt road and keep left at a junction as signposted. A **goat farm** lies to the left, but turn right at two more junctions to walk away from it. The track rises gently through a wooded valley with attractive rocky pinnacles above. Reach yet another track junction at **Ispidinie**, at 140m (460ft), and turn right.

Cross a river and walk up to a junction, turning left as signposted for 'Sentiero Paule Munduge'. The track climbs and bends, passing the ruins of **Dispensa Su Carcinargiu** and a picnic site at Fonte Su Carcinargiu, at 230m (755ft). The bendy, stony track climbs to a junction. Keep right, in effect straight ahead, reaching a signpost on a shoulder at **Cambarbu**, at 340m (1115ft).

Turn left to follow a rugged, but obvious path up through macchia and woodland. This drops for a couple of short stretches, then there are cliffs ahead. Climb and drift left to find and exploit a breach. Climb steeply past outcrops and jammed boulders in dense woods. Later, there are glimpses of the plains and

Granite slabs and pinnacles are passed on the way down steep, wooded slopes

distant sea. Climb among dense holm oaks and cross a couple of circular charcoal-burning hearths, levelling out and reaching a small, shallow lake, although in summer this may be an area of mud or baked clay. This is **Paule Munduge**, at 560m (1835ft), and a left turn leads to a map-board and picnic area.

Follow the path onwards, catching brief glimpses of the pool, then climb a rough and cobbly path. Cross a wooded gap and zigzag down a steep, bouldery slope into a wooded valley with rocky pinnacles above it. The path has chunky stone steps at first, then winds steep and stony down past a series of small charcoal-burning hearths. There are occasional views across to Talana and Monte Olinie. Walk down onto slopes of scrub woodland and cork oaks, then make a sharp right turn to land on a track near a river and a signpost. Turn left to return to the start, or right to continue to Predu Orrubiu.

Extension to Predu Orrubiu (5km/3 miles return)

Turn right to follow the track gently uphill, always flanked by trees and bushes, but often with a view far up through the valley, taking in the mountains that flank it. Don't be drawn left towards the river, but keep climbing gently to reach another ruined dispensa at

Predu Orrubiu, at 248m (814ft). This is the end of the waymarked trail, but the track continues further, splitting again and again in a rugged, remote, well-wooded area. Turn around and follow the track all the way back to Ponte de Irgeriai.

WALK 21
Santa Maria Navarrese and Monte Oro

Distance	15km or (including Monte Oro) 17km (9½ or 10½ miles)
Start/finish	Hotel Agugliastra, Santa Maria Navarrese
Total ascent/descent	800 or 1050m (2625 or 3445ft)
Time	4 or 5hrs
Map	IGMI 'Serie 50' 518 and 532, 'Serie 25' 518 III and 532 IV
Terrain	Narrow paths across scrub woodland slopes, with a climb to a rocky peak
Refreshment	Plenty of choice in Santa Maria Navarrese; bar/restaurant at Pedra Longa
Transport/access	Regular daily buses serve Santa Maria Navarrese from Lotzoraì, Tortolì and Baunei

Santa Maria Navarrese is a popular village, and many visitors follow a coastal path between it and the landmark rock tower of Pedra Longa. However, paths and tracks also allow explorations inland, offering a circuit around Monte Oro, and the option of climbing to the rocky summit.

Start in **Santa Maria Navarrese** at the Hotel Agugliastra. Follow the Viale Plammas up to a car park opposite a bar called Il Pozzo. Turn right up Via Pedra Longa, go round a steep bend, then left up the steep and narrow Via Montes Tundus. The end of the tarmac is reached at almost 200m (655ft). Turn right up a track, noting the spring of **Su Rele** above, and go through a gate. Turn left to walk up a track, which curves right as it climbs. Follow it up a slope of scrub woodland, but watch for a narrow path heading off to the left, which is usually marked by a cairn.

The path is often rugged, squeezing through wild olives, bushy lentisc and shrubby cistus, aided by paint marks. Limestone cliffs rise above, featuring a couple of prominent little caves. As height is gained the higher summit of **Montera Pittaine** comes into view, and euphorbia covers the slope. There are fine views south to the plains and coast. The path drops a little, then climbs, still rough and narrow, through the scrub. Follow a fence uphill and pass through dense arbutus, reaching a vehicle track around 420m (1380ft).

The track undulates gently round the steep and scrubby slopes of **Monte Scoine**. The peak is limestone, but the track crosses schist. For all its slight ups and downs, the track features a definite downward trend, followed by an upward trend. It heads down again to a junction with another track. At this point, the rocky peak of Monte Oro can be climbed as an extra.

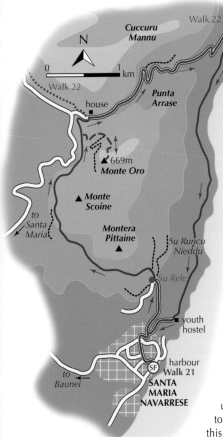

102

Ascent of Monte Oro (2km/1½ miles return)

Turn right up the track to a sharp right bend. Two paths head off to the left, close together. Take the second one, which is more obvious and stony, climbing a scrubby slope. It leads to a breach in an otherwise sheer cliff, blocked by a short fence, which is easily passed. Climb the most obvious trodden route, watching for little cairns and paint marks. The path drifts right, climbing a tongue of scree, and becomes more and more rocky. Keep climbing to the 669m (2195ft) summit of Monte Oro. Enjoy a splendid view, beyond the pepper-pot Monte Scione, to the coast and the lake of Stagno de Tortolì, with a plateau rising above Baunei and high mountains beyond. Retrace your steps back to the track junction.

Walk down the track, which becomes a patchy tarmac road leading down to another road beside a **house**. Turn right to follow the road past a spring-fed trough, down through a limestone-walled valley. The road features a number of bends, and eventually the prominent limestone tower of Pedra Longa comes into view. To visit the tower, walk down to a road-end car park, where a bar/restaurant might be open, or, to continue the walk, watch for the first 'P' sign for parking, seen from a road bend, and turn immediately right uphill.

A narrow, dusty, gravelly, stony path crosses a slope of limestone and scrub woodland. Cross a stream-bed and

Descending the stone-strewn slopes of Monte Oro using the only feasible breach

climb steps of schist. The idea is to stay on the most obvious path, generally around 100m (330ft) above the sea. The path runs more or less level, passing cistus, lentisc, wild olive and arbutus. The path rises and falls for short and long stretches. Cross a bouldery landslip and continue along a narrow path on a scrubby slope. Go down a steep, worn, dusty path, then climb a densely wooded slope. The path levels out and passes a junction. Climb past big limestone boulders, levelling out near a sign for **Su Runcu Nieddu**. Look back to see Pedra Longa and Punta Giradili, and look ahead to spot a harbour wall.

Views ahead are lost among dense arbutus. Note the transition from limestone to schist and back to limestone as the harbour wall comes into view again. Walk down a path with log steps to a car park, where there is a bar/restaurant and **youth hostel**, with a viewpoint overlooking the harbour and village of **Santa Maria Navarrese**. Follow the road gently downhill, then more steeply. It is the Via Pedra Longa, giving way to Viale Plammas, which leads back to the Hotel Agugliastra.

WALK 22
Baunei and Punta Giradili

Distance	16km (10 miles)
Start/finish	Baunei
Total ascent/descent	700m (2295ft)
Time	7hrs
Map	IGMI 'Serie 50' 517 and 518, IGMI 'Serie 25' 517 II and 518 III
Terrain	Extensive areas of macchia and steep, rocky slopes. Roads and tracks are used for much of the way, with steep and rugged linking paths.
Refreshment	Bars and restaurants in Baunei; bar/restaurant at Pedra Longa
Transport/access	Regular daily buses serve Baunei from Tortolì and Lotzoraì

The village of Baunei guards a road leading into an impressively wild and rugged region. Good tracks lead towards Punta Giradili, from where an old mule track clings to sheer cliffs, offering a remarkable route down to the coast. A road walk and forest track are used to return to Baunei.

Start near the church in **Baunei**, at 480m (1575ft), an attractive mountain village with plenty of services. A road is signposted uphill for 'Golgo', with several bends and junctions with other roads, but plenty of helpful signs throughout. Pines, cypress and holm oaks grow on a steep slope, and some cliffs and pinnacles are lashed with wire to prevent rock-falls. The road levels out above 650m (2130ft) on a broad, rolling plateau of broken limestone and macchia. This is the
Planu Supramonte, and the

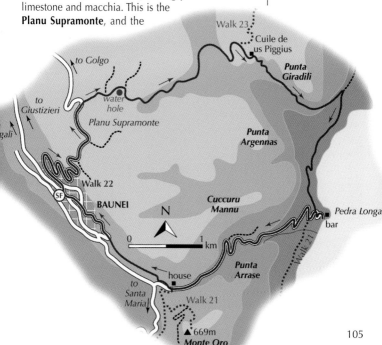

A single, narrow path slices across the cliff face of Punta Giradili

road winds onwards and gently downhill. A couple of tracks head off to the right, but take no notice of them. The macchia gives way to dense holm oak woods, then a **junction** is reached on a road bend.

Turn right to follow a track signposted for 'Punta Ginnirco', which heads gently down past macchia and woodland. There are a few other tracks, but stay on the main track. Holm oak, arbutus, juniper and lentisc are common. A feature of note is a **water hole** off to the right, built in an area that holds water after heavy rain. Just beyond it is a junction of tracks where a marker stone is located. Turn right here, then immediately fork left, following a track that winds gently down through a wooded valley.

There are no views at first, then the sheer cliff face of Punta Giradili is suddenly seen ahead. Stay on the main track, avoiding lesser ones to right and left, and the cliff is lost to sight. The track curves round the valley and starts to climb. ▸ Turn right down a track, crossing a rugged stile beside a gate. Don't follow the track when it swings left up to the wooden palisade of goat pens at **Cuile de us Piggius**. Instead, walk straight ahead down a grassy track. Before the track reaches a building tucked under a cliff, turn right down a steep, stony, winding path, reaching the undercut base of a cliff on **Punta Giradili**.

Walk 23 starts here.

An old mule track exploits a friable bed of limestone. Follow the path faithfully, watching for blue paint marks or small cairns. The rock tower of Pedra Longa is sometimes in view, but it takes a while to reach and there are no short-cuts. The path later goes through a gate and reaches its most remarkable stretch, making a traverse with sheer cliffs above and below, yet with little sense of exposure. Later, pass through a gap between massive boulders. Pick a way down scree and broken rock, covered in lentisc and juniper scrub. Keep an eye open for blue paint marks and small cairns in order to locate the only breach between the higher and lower cliffs.

Continue down a narrow, stony, dusty path through dense macchia. The path drifts left, away from Pedra Longa, but turn right where a path goes beneath the

Pedra Longa and Punta Giradili seen from a cruise along the Ogliastra coastline

Pedra Longa and Punta Giradili seen from a cruise along the Ogliastra coastline

boughs of a tree. Later, water is heard in a thicket, and while it can be approached, note that the path turns left, steeply downhill, beforehand. Eventually, a clearer path is reached, where there should be cairns. Turn right to follow its rugged course, crossing a stream, with the path gradually becoming easier to follow. There are striking views back to Punta Giradili, which seems to change shape every few paces. The path climbs through macchia, goes through a gate at the base of a cliff, then cuts across a steep, crumbling, stony slope to reach a road bend. Turn left down the road only if you wish to take a closer look at **Pedra Longa** or visit a bar/restaurant.

Otherwise, turn right up the road, taking all its bends as they come and reaching a **house** at the top of the valley before the road runs through a cutting to join the main road. Just after the house, turn right up a track, then when the track bends right, keep straight ahead along another track. This runs across a slope of pines, parallel to the main road. When a junction is reach, turn left to walk down a track to a road bend. A left turn on the bend leads down to the main road at a cemetery and bus stop on the edge of Baunei. A right turn, however, leads uphill, levelling out to enter **Baunei**. If this route is chosen, follow roads down into the village. Via G Deledda leads down to Via Orientale Sarda, where a right turn leads to the centre.

WALK 23
Irbidossili and Cala Goloritzè

Distance	17km (10½ miles)
Start/finish	near Cuile de us Piggius
Total ascent/descent	960m (3150ft)
Time	5hrs
Map	IGMI 'Serie 50' 518, 'Serie 25' 518 III and 518 IV
Terrain	Good tracks at the start and finish, with steep and rugged paths in between, often on well-wooded slopes
Refreshment	None
Transport/access	Buses run no closer than Baunei. For access by car from Baunei, take the road and track described as a walking route in Walk 22 as far as the turning for Cuile de us Piggius (parking is extremely limited). Adventurous drivers could continue to Irbidossili, but this stretch is described on foot.

This walk includes dramatic scenery, with some steep and rocky slopes. Providing walkers tread with care, they can enjoy a bird's-eye view of Cala Goloritzè and the pinnacle of Aguglia. This walk links with Walk 24, which offers a descent to the beach.

Don't walk to Cuile de us Piggius, but follow the main track uphill, passing through a broad gap between two rocky hills covered in macchia and tree scrub, around 790m (2590ft). The track undulates onwards and a **water hole** might be noticed down to the right. Later, there is a fenced **goat pen** on the left. After passing tall holm oaks, the track runs level, then gently uphill, then down a few steep bends. Holm oaks obscure views as the track rises, falls and levels out across limestone pavement. Go down a bendy stretch of track, passing a stone marked 'Irbidossili' (left) and 'Salinas Escursionisti' (right). Left leads to bare limestone at **Irbidossili**, where a stockade-like enclosure surrounds a farm, around 650m (2130ft). ◄ Turn right, however, to continue walking to Punta Salinas.

Follow a track down a slope of arbutus and tall

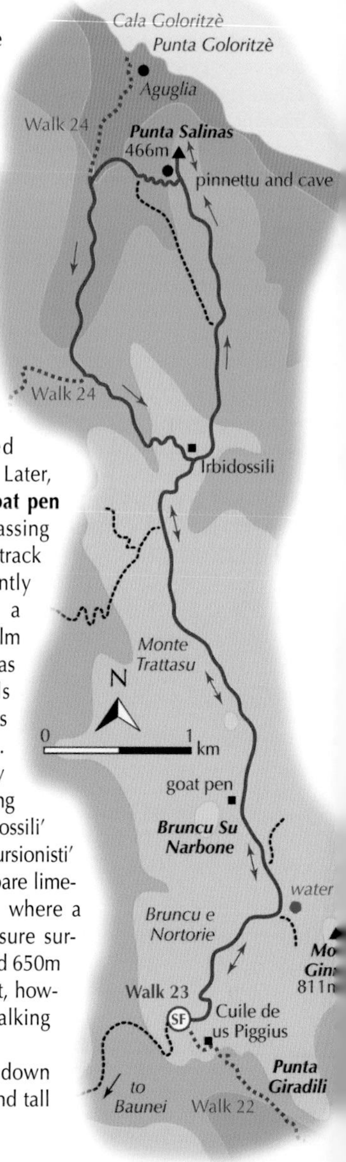

Parking here saves walking 10km (6¼ miles) in total.

Cala Goloritzè
Punta Goloritzè
● *Aguglia*
Walk 24
Punta Salinas
466m ▲
● *pinnettu and cave*
Walk 24
■ *Irbidossili*
Monte Trattasu
N
0   1 km
goat pen
Bruncu Su Narbone
water
Bruncu e Nortorie
Mo Gin 811m
Walk 23
SF *Cuile de us Piggius*
to Baunei Walk 22
Punta Giradili

110

holm oaks, passing a field. For
a moment there is a view ahead
to the top of Punta Salinas, but
watch carefully for a track junction. Keep right to follow the track
uphill, swinging left to roughly
follow the limestone crest. When
the track ends, continue along a
narrow path through tree scrub.
Pass a bulbous outcrop and a pinnettu, following the path onwards
with care as it becomes steep and
stony as it runs against a cliff. Look
down to spot a **pinnettu** and **cave**,
then stop before the path ends
abruptly on a cliff near the top of
Punta Salinas, at 466m (1529ft). A
splendid view looks down on Cala
Goloritzè and the incredible pinnacle of Aguglia.

Double back along the path,
watching for a short and easy
scramble down to the right, onto
broken rock, scree and wooded
areas. Zigzag down and look

*Looking down from
Punta Salinas to the
pinnacle of Aguglia, a
favourite with climbers*

back uphill to catch a glimpse of the pinnettu and cave,
seen earlier. Further downhill, tall holm oaks and massive
boulders are passed, then a path is reached. Turn right to
follow it downhill, crossing the bottom of a valley a few
times. Leave the valley on a gentle rising traverse across
a steep, wooded slope. The path rises and falls, joining
a well-trodden path that runs between Golgo and Cala
Goloritzè. (To visit Cala Goloritzè, turn right downhill,
referring to Walk 24. Return to this point continue Walk
23. The distance there and back is 2km/1¼ miles.)

Turn left uphill, passing a huge holm oak, where
rocks are arranged into seats. Climb past cave dwellings
and cross a gravelly, dusty slope, where there is a stand of
tall holm oaks. Just before the main path bends right on its
way to Golgo, climb left up a narrower path on a gravelly

111

slope covered in cistus. The aim is to navigate through a network of narrow paths, finding one that climbs roughly up the bed of a little valley. Locate this path while still among cistus and low tree scrub. It would be difficult to find later among tall, dense holm oaks and arbutus.

Pass a couple of charcoal-burning hearths and watch for a path climbing left. There may be a small cairn and a red paint blob. The path runs diagonally up a slope, mainly on scree at first, then later mostly on rock, but always walkable. At the top a little fence and gateway fill a gap between outcrops of rock. Go through the gap and down a slope of stones and slabs to return to **Irbidossili**. Turn right up the track to return to **Cuile de us Piggius**.

WALK 24
Golgo and Cala Goloritzè

Distance	9km (5½ miles)
Start/finish	Su Porteddu, Golgo
Total ascent/descent	550m (1805ft)
Time	3hrs
Map	IGMI 'Serie 50' 518, 'Serie 25' 518 III and 518 IV
Terrain	Well-wooded, rugged limestone with a clear, obvious, rough and stony path
Refreshment	Snack bar near the start at Su Porteddu
Transport/access	Buses run no closer than Baunei. For access by car, follow the tarmac road from Baunei towards San Pietro, and Golgo is reached before that point. Turn right as signposted for 'Su Porteddu' and 'Cala Goloritzè'. There is room to park a few cars at just over 400m (1315ft).

This classic walk is relatively short and blessed with dramatic scenery. As a result it is also very popular, and the tiny beach of Cala Goloritzè can get very busy, so avoid weekends and holidays. It is possible to arrange to be collected by boat from Cala Goloritzè, but otherwise the return is a climb back inland to Golgo.

From the signposted junction at **Golgo** either follow the winding track onwards on foot or drive along it to a fenced compound, where another car park is available, along with a campsite, near a snack bar at **Su Porteddu**. Don't enter the compound unless you want to use its facilities, but pass a barrier and follow the track onwards into woodland to continue walking. Watch out for a path on the left, marked 'Goloritzè' on a stone. The initial climb is at a gentle gradient, but the path is rough, rocky and stony. The limestone slope bears holm oak, juniper and lentisc, with a ground cover of cistus, rock rose and asphodel. The path levels out on a broad gap at 471m (1545ft).

As the descent begins, there is often more rock than vegetation, with a brief glimpse down to the sea and to a striking pinnacle, which the route passes later. Follow the path as it makes a slight climb, crossing a crystalline band before heading down past a few stout holm oaks. Pass a few cave dwellings, noting how the valley ahead is flanked by sheer limestone cliffs. There is a sudden view of the pinnacle again. Pass a huge holm oak where rocks

Not a cave, but a natural arch formed where a monstrous boulder leans against a cliff

Walk 23 joins on the right nearby.

are arranged into seats. ◀ Much further down the path, an enormous boulder is wedged against a cliff, leaving a large triangular passage for the path. Later, the path passes a striking overhang, and there is another view of the pinnacle. Dense woodland obscures views, then the path passes the base of the incredible pinnacle of **Aguglia**.

Chunky stone steps feature a fence for protection on the final descent to **Cala Goloritzè**. Limestone gravel is lapped by a blue-green sea, and this can be a very popular beach, despite its small size. Explorations are limited, due to massive boulders and sheer cliffs. Unless a pick-up has been arranged by boat, return to the start by retracing your steps.

WALK 25

Serra Ovara and Cala Sisine

Distance	18km or (to Cala Sisine) 20.5km (11 or 12½ miles)
Start/finish	Urele, beyond San Pietro
Total ascent/descent	700m (2295ft)
Time	7hrs
Map	IGMI 'Serie 50' 517, 'Serie 25' 517 I
Terrain	A narrow path up a broad, rocky, wooded crest. An awkward descent requires careful route-finding. An easy valley track to finish.
Refreshment	Bar/restaurant at Cala Sisine
Transport/access	Buses run no closer than Baunei. For access by car follow the road from Baunei to Golgo and San Pietro. When the tarmac ends, follow the rugged dirt road. Take the junction signposted to 'Cala Sisine'. Pass a muddy pool (or baked mud) to reach a junction. Turn right and park as soon as possible off the track at Urele.

Many people wander down through a canyon-like valley to Cala Sisine, but few realise that there are paths over the hills alongside. An interesting path runs along the crest of Serra Ovara to link with a little-known path that descends into the Codula Sisine gorge, but both require careful route-finding.

At **Urele**, around 300m (985ft), look ahead up the track to see a sheepfold on the hillside – it is important not to pass it. Instead, watch for a rough and rocky path to the right of the track, climbing into macchia. Within moments there is a view of the sea, and while the path may be narrow, it is fairly obvious throughout. Pass juniper, holm oak, lentisc and cistus. There is only one junction, where a right turn is made to keep climbing. The gradient is gentle, with a few zigzags. Some stretches are level and gravelly, while others are rocky or well wooded. If the path is lost, always retrace steps to locate it.

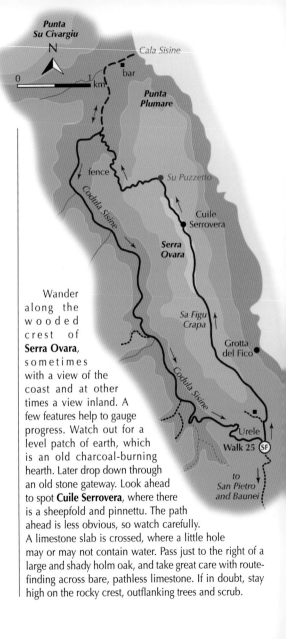

Wander along the wooded crest of **Serra Ovara**, sometimes with a view of the coast and at other times a view inland. A few features help to gauge progress. Watch out for a level patch of earth, which is an old charcoal-burning hearth. Later drop down through an old stone gateway. Look ahead to spot **Cuile Serrovera**, where there is a sheepfold and pinnettu. The path ahead is less obvious, so watch carefully. A limestone slab is crossed, where a little hole may or may not contain water. Pass just to the right of a large and shady holm oak, and take great care with route-finding across bare, pathless limestone. If in doubt, stay high on the rocky crest, outflanking trees and scrub.

Following a path over the remote and rugged crest of Serra Ovara

Watch for a gravel path onto a gap on the crest, then search for **Su Puzzetto**, a distinctive little water hole partly covered by juniper logs. To confirm it turn left, and a small artificial water catchment is seen at the foot of a limestone cliff. ▶

From the water catchment, head directly west to pass a large hollow in the limestone. In fact, it is best to drop into the hollow, where there is a deep sink-hole. Now, imagine that the hollow was brim-full of water, and climb over a rocky lip to see where the water would spill. There is nothing in sight except steep, bare rock leading down to dense macchia. Pick a way carefully down the rock slope and look carefully for a breach in the macchia. A hidden path is revealed, zigzagging downhill – quite obvious once located. If it cannot be found, do not proceed, but retrace your steps.

The stony path is marked with occasional small cairns, and lesser paths should not be followed. On a densely wooded slope, the path is marked by occasional stones lodged in the branches of small trees, usually at eye-level. The path drifts to the right across a densely wooded little

If route-finding has been difficult so far, you should perhaps at this point retrace your steps back to the start, as the descent needs even more care.

valley, reaching a small **fence** of juniper logs. Pass through a small gap and follow the path down a slope that becomes steep, stony and well wooded, followed by loose scree. Watch for a path on the right, leaving the scree, dropping further to pass beneath an overhanging cliff.

Another scree leads downhill, but watch carefully for the path, especially where it heads left and has a built-up edge. Cross a densely wooded slope, with occasional views down to a broad, stony and usually dry riverbed. Follow the path faithfully, passing a couple of charcoal-burning hearths before suddenly landing on a track in **Codula Sisine**. There are no further route-finding difficulties and the rest of the walk is easy. ◀ Either turn right for the bar and beach at **Cala Sisine**, returning later (2.5km/1½ miles return), or turn left to return to Urele.

Walk 12 is met here.

Turning left, the track quickly reaches the stony riverbed. Cross over it and pick up the track on the other

A long and easy walk climbs gradually through the gorge of Codula Sisine

side, passing a barrier. Beyond this point, an occasional vehicle might be encountered on the track, otherwise keep crossing and recrossing the riverbed, admiring the bare cliffs and steep, wooded slopes throughout. There are also two other tracks, both on the right, so keep left at both junctions.

Eventually, the track climbs from the riverbed, from about 150m (490ft), and is steep and stone-paved. Pass a small picnic site in a wooded area, then there is another stone-paved stretch with a fence alongside. Later, in a more open area of scrub, a short-cut is available up a narrow path on the left. If this is missed, then simply turn left at the next track junction to return to Urele.

WALK 26
Genna Sesole to Golgo

Distance	13km (8 miles)
Start	Genna Sesole
Finish	Su Porteddu, Golgo
Total ascent	210m (690ft)
Total descent	500m (1640ft)
Time	4hrs
Map	IGMI 'Serie 50' 517 and 518, 'Serie 25' 517 I and 518 III
Terrain	Good tracks and rugged riverbeds in well-wooded valleys
Refreshment	Bar/restaurants at Coop Goloritzè and Su Porteddu
Transport/access	Infrequent daily buses pass Genna Sesole (on Baunei–Giustizieri route). Tell the driver in advance to stop on a bend between two tunnels, where the walk begins. Miss this stop and your plans for the day are ruined. There is no transport to or from the finish at Golgo.

For walkers without cars, this route offers an interesting link between a bus route and the Golgo plateau. The incredible mountain road between Baunei and Giustizieri has been hacked from cliffs and is often covered to protect it from rock-falls. Here in the heart of the Golgo plateau, with no transport away, the assumption is that you will be staying to enjoy more walks, either lodging at Coop Goloritzè or camping at Su Porteddu.

At **Genna Sesole** there is only a road bend between two tunnels, a parking space, and access down to a forested area and uphill for Golgo. Walk up a track and note the hard and soft layers in the limestone, which causes land-slips and rock-falls. A short climb leads into holm oak woods, and on reaching a fork keep walking ahead and downhill. The bendy track runs through dense woods, with occasional views of nearby cliffs. Stay on the main track at all times, crossing and recrossing the

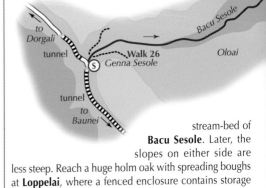

stream-bed of **Bacu Sesole**. Later, the slopes on either side are less steep. Reach a huge holm oak with spreading boughs at **Loppelai**, where a fenced enclosure contains storage tanks.

Tracks lead left and right, so keep right, winding and undulating through the woods. One descent passes

The bare limestone bed of Bacu Loppelai, where a track climbs up to Golgo

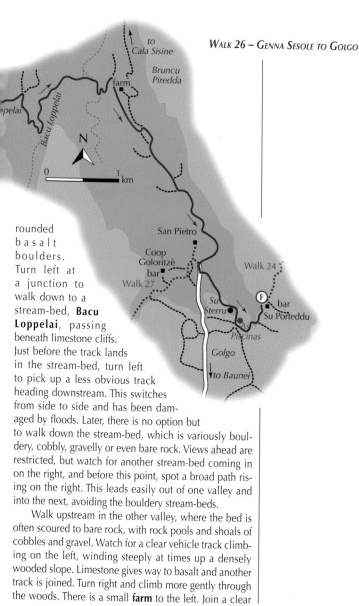

rounded basalt boulders. Turn left at a junction to walk down to a stream-bed, **Bacu Loppelai**, passing beneath limestone cliffs. Just before the track lands in the stream-bed, turn left to pick up a less obvious track heading downstream. This switches from side to side and has been damaged by floods. Later, there is no option but to walk down the stream-bed, which is variously bouldery, cobbly, gravelly or even bare rock. Views ahead are restricted, but watch for another stream-bed coming in on the right, and before this point, spot a broad path rising on the right. This leads easily out of one valley and into the next, avoiding the bouldery stream-beds.

Walk upstream in the other valley, where the bed is often scoured to bare rock, with rock pools and shoals of cobbles and gravel. Watch for a clear vehicle track climbing on the left, winding steeply at times up a densely wooded slope. Limestone gives way to basalt and another track is joined. Turn right and climb more gently through the woods. There is a small **farm** to the left. Join a clear

121

dirt road and turn right, keeping right at a junction which is signposted back for 'Cala Sisine'. Continue onwards to reach another junction near the chapel of **San Pietro**.

Leave the chapel and walk back along the track, through the gateway in the drystone wall. Turn left to reach a well-signposted junction, where left is for Cala Sisine and right is for Baunei. Turn right and follow the dirt road halfway towards where it turns to tarmac. Just after passing a fine, solitary cork oak, turn left along a track. Fork right, then later left, to reach a fenced enclosure, a notice and a viewpoint into an impressive cave at **Su Sterru**.

Keep left of the enclosure to follow a well-worn path flanked by cistus, weaving between basalt boulders, flanked by rustic fencing. Stay close to the fencing to be guided to little water holes in the basalt at **As Piscinas**. Walk straight ahead to reach a junction of tracks. Turn left to reach a campsite and bar/restaurant at **Su Porteddu**, at just over just over 400m (1315ft). ◀

There is immediate access to Walk 24 to Cala Goloritzè.

WALK 27
Genna Ramene to Golgo

Distance	8km (5 miles)
Start	Genna Ramene
Finish	Su Porteddu, Golgo
Total ascent	10m (30ft)
Total descent	200m (655ft)
Time	2hrs 30min
Map	IGMI 'Serie 50' 517 and 518, 'Serie 25' 517 I and 518 III
Terrain	Easy walking along a track through a well-wooded valley
Refreshment	Bar/restaurants at Coop Goloritzè and Su Porteddu
Transport/access	Infrequent daily buses pass Genna Ramene (Baunei–Giustizieri route). No transport to or from Golgo.

For walkers without cars, this is a short and easy approach to the Golgo plateau from a bus route. It is shorter than walking along the road from Baunei to Golgo, and easier than Walk 26. Walkers who base themselves at a simple lodging or campsite will have access to further walks in the area.

Start at a viewpoint at **Genna Ramene**, at 600m (1970ft). Walk down the road in the direction of Baunei and turn left up a clear track through scrub woodland containing holm oak, arbutus, heather and cistus. The track swings left as it descends, crossing the stream-bed of **Bacu Dolcolce** in a valley bottom. Keep right to follow the track, crossing the stream-bed repeatedly, passing tall holm oak and arbutus, with

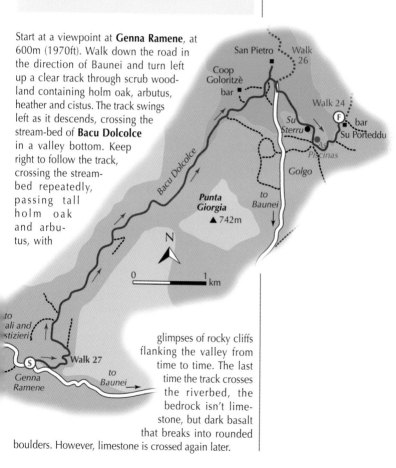

glimpses of rocky cliffs flanking the valley from time to time. The last time the track crosses the riverbed, the bedrock isn't limestone, but dark basalt that breaks into rounded boulders. However, limestone is crossed again later.

123

Basalt lies on top of limestone at Golgo, where waterholes are used by animals

There is an option to turn left along a track to **Coop Goloritzè** and Il Rifugio bar/restaurant, but otherwise keep straight ahead. Pass a plain dotted with trees, grazed for centuries by goats, pigs, donkeys and horses. Turn left at a junction, signposted for 'Chiesa San Pietro Maneggio'. Pass two wells and turn right, going through a gateway in a drystone wall to reach **San Pietro**. The church stands inside a walled enclosure with a refuge alongside. Huge gnarled trees shade stone seats nearby.

Leave the church and walk back along the track, through the gateway in the drystone wall. Turn left to reach a well-signposted junction, where left is for Cala Sisine and right is for Baunei. Turn right and follow the dirt road halfway towards where it turns to tarmac. Just after passing a fine, solitary cork oak, turn left along a track. Fork right, then later left, to reach a fenced enclosure, a notice and a viewpoint into an impressive cave at **Su Sterru**.

Keep left of the enclosure to follow a well-worn path flanked by cistus, weaving between basalt boulders, flanked by rustic fencing. Stay close to the fencing to be

guided to little water holes in the basalt at **As Piscinas**.
Walk straight ahead to reach a junction of tracks. Turn left
to reach a campsite and bar/restaurant at **Su Porteddu**, at
just over just over 400m (1315ft). ▸

There is immediate
access to Walk 24 to
Cala Goloritzè.

WALK 28
Triei and Osono

Distance	16km (10 miles)
Start/finish	Triei
Total ascent/descent	475m (1560ft)
Time	5hrs
Map	IGMI 'Serie 50' 517, 'Serie 25' 517 II
Terrain	Minor roads and forest tracks, although some short sections are very rough and stony
Refreshment	A few bars at Triei
Transport/access	Regular daily buses serve Triei from Tortolì and Lotzoraì

Triei is an interesting mountain village, brightened
by strange murals and sculptures, and handy for
this circular walk. The route passes springs and
archaeological sites while wandering around
sparsely forested granite and schist hills. Much of
the route is on easy forest tracks, but some parts are
rugged, having suffered storm damage.

Start in **Triei** by walking downhill and follow the main
road out of the village. Turn right up a road signposted
for two springs – 'Sorgente Natural Bau Nuraxi' and
'Sorgente Natural Osono'. Walk up the road, keep
straight ahead at one junction, then turn right at another,
again signposted for the springs. Reach a stony riverbed
where there are stone walls and a parking space. Steps
lead down to **Sorgente Bau Nuraxi**, beneath a carob
tree.

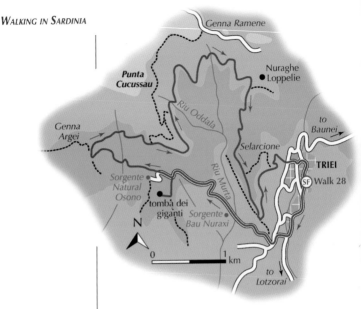

Follow the road onwards and upwards, passing a building while noticing vines and little hayfields among woods and macchia. The road zigzags up a slope of crumbling granite, reaching a crest at almost 250m (820ft), where cistus spreads in all directions. A track on

An arc of granite slabs flank the portal to a passage grave, or tomba dei giganti

126

the left is signposted 'Tomba dei Giganti'. Walk down it and turn right at another signpost. Reach a large gate in a walled enclosure, where a semi-circular arrangement of granite slabs guards the entrance to a passage grave, or *tomba dei giganti*. Return to the road and turn left.

Further along the road, another left turn is signposted for **Sorgente Natural Osono**, down to another spring. (If this is visited, retrace your steps to the signpost.) Leave the road and walk straight along a track towards a pine forest and a jagged range of little mountains. Stout metal gates are passed as the track drops into the forest, then climbs past a few eucalyptus trees. Later, there is a pronounced right turn as the track climbs to a junction. Keep right again and climb more gently, passing occasional mimosa trees. The pine forest is patchy, with abundant cistus and rock-rose.

The track rises gently and leaves the forest to cross a steep slope of macchia. There is a very definite left turn, where Triei is seen below and the village of Baunei is high above. A sloping plain stretches to the sea, where the headland at Arbatax is prominent. Arbutus grows on the slope as the track rises gently, reaching a junction of tracks beside three cork oaks. The main track swings sharp left uphill and is signposted for 'Genna Ramene'. Ahead are two tracks, one climbing left and one descending right.

Go down the track on the right, which looks grassy, but becomes rough and stony. It continues level and easy round a corner, then goes downhill rough and stony or on bare schist bedrock. Climb past a few cork oaks, while the gradient gradually eases and the surface improves. The track runs more or less level, grassy and flowery, later passing a fig tree. There are more rugged stretches, then an easier stretch round a ridge where a line of cork oaks grows alongside. Pass a rugged, scrubby hill crowned by a rocky outcrop where the collapsed, bouldery ruins **Nuraghe Loppelie** are located, but are difficult to reach.

Walk straight ahead down the track and Triei comes into view. Don't short-cut, but stay on the clearest track down a ridge of macchia with a few pines. There are sudden bends to right and left on the way down, and the second set of bends takes the track into denser pine forest. Keep to the main track, leaving the forest to pass a few figs, eucalyptus, olives and dense macchia. A track joins from the right, then further along turn left along another track, where there is a sudden view of Triei.

The track falls and rises gently, swings right towards the village and drops into a valley. Cross a riverbed and follow the track to the top end of **Triei**. At a road junction, turn left downhill to enter the village. Either follow a one-way (*senso unico*) sign, down a cobbled road on the right, or keep straight ahead to reach the bus stop and bars.

WALK 29
Perda Pera and Monte Arista

Distance	8km (5 miles)
Start/finish	Sa Spiaggetta, near Perda Pera
Total ascent/descent	400m (1310ft)
Time	3hrs
Map	IGMI 'Serie 50' 541, 'Serie 25' 541 I
Terrain	Steep and well-wooded paths, ending with an easy road walk
Refreshment	None
Transport/access	Buses run no closer than Cardeddu, 5km (3 miles) away. A car is useful to reach Perda Pera and a beach car park at Sa Spiaggetta.

Sa Spiaggetta is a popular beach near Perda Pera, itself near Cardeddu. Steep wooded slopes rise inland, notably to Monte Ferru, but the object of this walk is to climb high on the slopes of Monte Arista. A network of paths is hidden on densely wooded slopes, but route-finding is fairly straightforward.

From **Sa Spiaggetta** walk further along the road, but not as far as a sign reading 'Marino de Gairo'. Instead, leave the road at a gate and ladder-stile on the right, flashed with blue and yellow paint. Pass a transformer tower among lentisc bushes and follow a broad and obvious grassy path. Note a **pinnettu** up to the right. The path has a river to the left, in the valley of **Bau de Lispedda**, and granite outcrops to the right. Swing right later, climbing through a rocky notch, then head downhill.

Pass through a gateway in a fence, cross two streams, then go through another gateway. Climb across a couple more stream-beds, then take care among dense holm oaks where the path forks. Turn right as flashed blue/yellow. (The other path passes a 'sentiero' sign and reaches a four-way directional notice on a bushy gap at Arcu Niulu. If this is reached, retrace your steps to the junction.) There are no more markers, so be sure to stay on the most obvious trodden path. This links with a clear

Mist drifts off the sea, with the top of Monte Ferru staying clear

path offering a fine view back down the valley, followed by a steep and boulder-strewn climb through more dense woods. The path undulates and crosses a gap high on **Monte Arista**, around 350m (1150ft).

There is a view northwards along the coast before the path drops through woods. There are red/white markers and a 'sentiero' sign at a point where a lesser path heads left, so keep right to continue downhill. Eventually emerge from the woods at a pinnettu, **Cuile sa Dappara**, passing another 'sentiero' sign and a waterworks building. The track splits and either one can be followed. They both become concrete before joining for a steep descent to a road and houses at **Perda Pera**. Turn right and note the tumbled ruins of **Nuraghe de Perda Pera** up to the right. Simply follow the road back to **Sa Spiaggetta**.

WALK 30
Ulassai, Canyon and Punta Matzeu

Distance	8km or (with ascent of Punta Matzeu) 9km (5 or 5½ miles)
Start/finish	Comune (town hall), Ulassai
Total ascent/descent	450m (1475ft)
Time	3hrs
Map	IGMI 'Serie 50' 531, 'Serie 25' 531 II and III
Terrain	Some steep, rugged, wooded paths, as well as roads and tracks
Refreshment	Bars and restaurants in Ulassai
Transport/access	Regular daily buses serve Ulassai from Lanusei, Jerzu and Taquisara
Note	Route uses waymarked trails 502 and 503

Ulassai is a compact village clinging to a very steep slope, with sheer limestone cliffs above. Two short loop walks from the village centre are here combined into a route abounding in dramatic scenery. The 'canyon' is very popular with rock climbers, while Punta Matzeu is a remarkable viewpoint.

Start at the comune (town hall) in the centre of **Ulassai**, where there is a mapboard. Walk up the nearby stone-paved Via Venezia to a supermarket. Turn right up Via Plebiscito and continue up Via Bosa. Climb a flight of steps beside a church to reach a building housing an art form called Lavatoio. Turn left up a stone-paved road, sharp right up another stone-paved road, then left and right, zigzagging up broad, buttressed ramps that are concrete, grassy and stony. Level out and drop to the end of a grassy ramp, then follow a narrow, stony path to the **canyon**.

Pass a cave beneath a huge boulder leaning against a cliff. Squeeze under another boulder, then climb between massive boulders jammed in the bottom of the canyon, using crude stone steps, verging on scrambling. Cross a crest between rock walls and descend more easily. Keep to the left-hand side to follow a path, as the right-hand side features remarkably deep clefts. The path runs up and down stone steps, then descends into a rugged, mixed woods. Turn right at a path junction as signposted for 'Marosini'.

The path drops among woods and rocks, apart from a few paces uphill. Go down through a very narrow rocky cleft, with low headroom and rock-steps at the bottom. Walk along a level limestone terrace path into mixed woods. Turn sharp right down a clear woodland path, always walking ahead and downhill, except when forced to zigzag. Wind down between monstrous boulders to reach a road bend. Turn right and follow the road above a **cemetery** to reach the first houses in **Ulassai**.

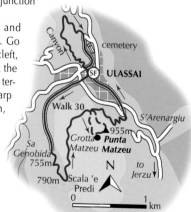

Turn right up the stone-paved Via Santa Croce to a point above the church. Walk down steps to the supermarket and turn right through a stone arch. Keep to the left side of a green, following a concrete road to the left of a play-park and sports ground. This gives way to a disintegrating tarmac road, which later climbs beneath unstable cliffs that drop large rocks. The tarmac ends, and a track reaches locked gates. Keep left along an obvious, almost level path, with fine views across the valley to Walk 31, from slopes of holm oak, arbutus, juniper, lentisc and heather.

Turn left at **Sa Genobida**, at 755m (2475ft), where a signpost points up chunky stone steps on the wooded slope. At a higher level a limestone terrace leads to an area of bare earth and stones completely turned over by pigs at **Scala 'e Predi**, at 790m (2590ft). Turn left up a stony path through woods, passing a signpost for S'Arenargiu. The rugged path climbs to a junction, so keep right and level out among holm oaks. Descend past another junction and keep ahead down the broadest and clearest track, later passing a signpost. Walk ahead a short way to another signpost, closely followed by yet another signpost. These offer two options to turn right for Punta Matzeu.

Ascent of Punta Matzeu (1km/½ mile return)

Turn right at the first of the two signposts close together, and right again at another signpost for Punta Matzeu. The path is bare rock at first, with little rock-steps later, then a gentle and easy stretch. Turn left uphill at a junction, reaching a signpost for Grotta Matzeu. (This cave lies to the right and is easily visited.) Turn left up a rugged path that becomes a winding stone stairway to the summit of Punta Matzeu, at 955m (3133ft).

Scout around for remarkable views from the mountains to the coast, including the villages of Jerzu, Ulassai, Osini and Gairo Sant Elena. To descend, take care locating a path scrambling down through rocky clefts. Continue down a steep wooded slope, turning right at the bottom.

The path returning to Ulassia goes down rugged stone steps, crosses a drystone wall and exploits a bushy terrace with cliffs above and below. After an undulating stretch, zigzag downhill without short-cuts on a slope of schist to reach a track and signpost at **S'Arenargiu**, at 695m (2280ft). Turn left to follow a concrete road past a textile works called Tessile to reach a tarmac road bend. Either follow the road left uphill, or right downhill, to return to **Ulassai**.

View from the edge of Punta Matzeu, taking in Ulassai and the mountains far beyond

WALK 31

Ulassai and Baulassa

Distance	15km or (from Ulassai) 19km (9½ or 12 miles)
Start/finish	Grotte Su Marmuri
Alternative start/finish	Comune (town hall), Ulassai
Total ascent/descent	350 or 500m (1150 or 1640ft)
Time	6 or 7hrs
Map	IGMI 'Serie 50' 531, 'Serie 25' 531 III
Terrain	Rugged woodland paths, as well as easy tracks and roads

Refreshment	Bars and restaurants in Ulassai
Transport/access	Regular daily buses serve Ulassai from Lanusei, Jerzu and Taquisara. Motorists can drive to the start by following bendy roads signposted for 'Grotte Su Marmuri' and 'Parking' before reaching a show-cave. Walkers are likely to start at the town hall in Ulassai.
Note	Route uses waymarked trail 505

This convoluted circuit, the Sentiero Su Marmuri, around well-wooded limestone hills wanders from one splendid cliff-top viewpoint to another, reaching secluded picnic sites at Sa Canna and Baulassa. The show-cave of Grotte Su Marmuri can be visited if open. There is an option to link with Walk 32, but this would result in a very long day's trek.

From the comune (town hall) in **Ulassai**, where there is a mapboard, walk up the nearby stone-paved Via Venezia to a supermarket. Turn right up Via Plebiscito and

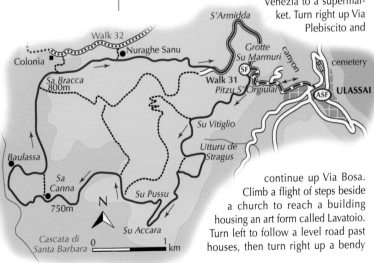

continue up Via Bosa. Climb a flight of steps beside a church to reach a building housing an art form called Lavatoio. Turn left to follow a level road past houses, then turn right up a bendy road until a gravel car park is reached before **Grotte Su Marmuri**, at 800m (2625ft). ▶

A rough and rocky path leaves the car park, signposted for 'Pitzu S' Orgiulai'. Climb through holm oak and juniper close to a cliff edge. Cross a ladder-stile and later level out. Any paths heading left offer views over the cliff edge, some signposted as viewpoints (*punto panoramico*) – after having a look, retrace your steps and continue along the main path. A signposted junction is reached at **Pitzu S' Orgiulai**, at 930m (3050ft), and further along the main path, fork left. The path becomes broad and clear, either with views or in dense woods, and reaches a signposted junction at **Su Vitiglio**, at 910m (2985ft). Walk a short way ahead up a broad path to reach a junction with a clearer track.

Turn left as signposted, through a barrier gate and gently down to another junction and signpost at **Utturu de Stragus**, at 920m (3020ft). Turn left up another track among tall holm oaks, then right as signposted along a rugged woodland path. At the next signpost, a punto panoramico is noted as being 5 minutes away, but a cliff edge is reached after 5 seconds! The path climbs and exploits a terrace with cliffs above and below, then broadens as it drops through woods. Turn left along a track, fork left at a junction, climbing gently, and later fork right along a lesser track. Turn right shortly afterwards down a track, turning sharp right and later winding steeply down through woods. Level out and keep straight ahead at a junction, with views down a valley as the path rises beside a slight rocky edge at **Su Pussu**.

Cross a gentle, well-wooded gap and keep left at a junction. Drop steeply, with less holm oak and more pine, juniper, arbutus and cistus. Keep straight ahead at a signposted junction, catching a valley view before heading back into woods and winding down to a junction at **Sa Canna**, at 750m (2460ft), where there is a picnic site. ▶

Walk past the picnic site, admiring tall alder trees beside a stream, and turn left along a narrow woodland path signposted for 'Sa Bracca'. This runs through woods,

The start point for the shorter route is at Grotte Su Marmuri.

There is an option to detour to a viewpoint overlooking Cascata di Santa Barbara, but it is difficult to see the waterfall.

bushy scrub and stony areas. Pass or cross a small concrete aqueduct, and later follow a stream in a plantation of pines, reaching a track beside a culvert bridge. Turn right to reach **Baulassa**, around 750m (2460ft), where there are a picnic site and a couple of pinnettus thatched with holm oak.

The bendy track rises through mixed forest, and the route lies straight ahead at a junction, and straight ahead at another junction. A long, gentle ascent through mixed forest and undergrowth leads to another junction. Turn left and climb gently, keeping straight ahead past a junction at **Sa Bracca**, at 800m (2625ft). ◄ Follow the track onwards, avoiding a couple of lesser paths to the left. However, watch for the restored **Nuraghe Sanu** on the left, in a fenced enclosure.

Later, keep straight ahead at a track junction, rising gently and winding up a rugged slope of holm oaks. Short stretches are stone-paved or concrete, and the track reaches a minor road and a signpost. Turn left up the bendy road, which undulates and has one good viewpoint. It drops through woods to pass the show-cave of **Grotte Su Marmuri**, and all that remains is the optional continuation to **Ulassai**.

A left turn offers a link with Walk 32.

Nuraghe Sanu stands in a fenced enclosure, and it can also be visited on Walk 32

WALK 32
Osini and Nuraghe Serbissi

Distance	16km or (from Osini) 24km (10 or 15 miles)
Start/finish	Pitzu 'e Taccu
Alternative start/finish	Osini
Total ascent/descent	350 or 650m (1150 or 2130ft)
Time	5 or 7hrs
Map	IGMI 'Serie 50' 531, 'Serie 25' 531 III
Terrain	Mostly along roads and clear tracks through well-wooded hills
Refreshment	Bars and restaurants in Osini
Transport/access	Motorists can drive up through Scala di San Giorgio to Pitzu 'e Taccu, but walkers who reach Osini by bus (regular daily services from Jerzu, Ulassai, Lanusei and Taquisara) have to walk there.
Note	Route uses waymarked trail 521

The road from Osini goes by way of the Scala di San Giorgio – a remarkable cleft in a line of cliffs that gives access to the well-wooded hills beyond. Four nuraghic towers are linked on this route, with Nuraghe Serbissi being in an excellent state of preservation high above Taquisara.

Start in the middle of **Osini** and go round the back of the *carabinieri* (police station). Climb steps and go through an arch to pass the old railway station, now a dwelling. Climb more steps to reach Via Sardegna and turn right to follow the road out of the village. This crosses a well-wooded slope and passes a football ground, then tight bends climb into a rock-walled valley. There is a hairpin bend at **Scala di San Giorgio**, where exciting paths and stone steps lead to amazing viewpoints. ▸ The road rises and falls, reaching a fork at **Pitzu 'e Taccu**, at 885m (2905ft). The route heads left, and later returns on the

There is a charge, payable at a hut, and an extra hour should be allowed for this excursion.

137

right. (Motorists can use a small parking space and start walking here, saving 8km/5 miles.)

Fork left down the road, which is bendy on a slope of holm oaks, then a long, straight stretch runs through pine forest. **Nuraghe Orruttu** stands to the left at 820m (2690ft). Further along the road, round a couple of slight bends, **Nuraghe Sanu** stands further away to the left, along with a tomba dei giganti nearby. Continue along the road, keeping right of a large building at **Colonia**. Afterwards, a turning to the left links with Walk 31, but keep right along a track as signposted for 'Funtana Urceni'.

The track later makes a pronounced right turn, then at a junction, keep right (in effect, straight ahead). The surface is more rugged as the track climbs to another junction. Keep straight ahead, climb through mixed forest and note that **Funtana Urceni** lies just up to the right, at 850m (2790ft). Head left up the track, which becomes grassy, then rugged, then broken concrete, and finally

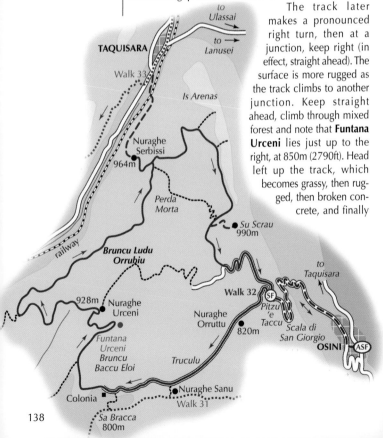

smooth concrete as it bends to reach a sign-posted junction. **Nuraghe Urceni** sits on top of a little cliff at 928m (3045ft). For a closer view, do not approach it directly, but turn right along a track, then left up a path. The tower is surrounded by inter-linked circular hut foundations. Double back to the track junction and follow the track signposted for 'Nuraghe Serbissi'.

The track winds and undulates gently, but generally climbs through mixed forest with occasional views. When a junction is reached, turn right up a stony track, crossing a rise and heading gently downhill. Views reveal a deep valley and Taquisara, with mountains beyond, all explored on Walk 33, while the prominent rock tower of Perda Liana is visited on Walk 34. Views are lost as the track forks left down into a broad valley, with woods and clearings. Keep left of a water store, and the track rises to join a clearer track. Turn left again, sharp right at a gravel parking space, then climb steeply up a track, concrete in parts, or use a rocky path running parallel.

Either way leads to **Nuraghe Serbissi**, at 964m (3160ft), where well-preserved nuraghic towers are surrounded by inter-linked circular hut foundations. The top of the main tower is a fine viewpoint. Explore the site fully, then retrace steps down past the car park and back along the

Nuraghe Serbissi is in an excellent state of preservation and is a splendid viewpoint

Alternatively, it is possible to visit Taquisara from Nuraghe Serbissi.

track. ◄ Walk straight ahead from a junction as signposted for 'Su Scrau' and 'Pitzu 'e Taccu'. The forest track rises and falls a bit, passes another signposted junction, and keeps left to climb further. After that, avoid tracks heading left, and stay on the main track. There are no signposts, only sparse red/white markers. Climb over a rise, down into a dip, then uphill again before the track undulates through woods. A concrete bend is reached at a junction. ◄

A left turn offers an optional climb to Su Scrau and a fire tower at 990m (3250ft). The distance there and back is 1km/½ mile.

Follow the track, now a dirt road, generally downhill to link with a tarmac road. Turn left to follow this bendy road, with views later down onto the road used earlier in the day. Return to the junction at **Pitzu 'e Taccu**, and if your car was parked here, then this is the finish. Otherwise keep walking, and any spare time can be used exploring Scala di San Giorgio on the way back to **Osini**.

WALK 33
Taquisara and Is Tostoinus

Distance	12km (7½ miles)
Start/finish	Taquisara
Total ascent/descent	300m (985ft)
Time	4hrs
Map	IGMI 'Serie 50' 531, 'Serie 25' 531 III
Terrain	Rugged hill paths, forest tracks and roads
Refreshment	Bar/restaurant at Taquisara
Transport/access	Regular daily buses serve Taquisara from Jerzu, Ullassai and Lanusei
Note	Route uses waymarked trail 102

Taquisara is a remote and sleepy little village with a summer railway service, the Trenino Verde. Outside of summer, buses or cars have to be used to reach it. The route follows a scenic and interesting circular walk, the Sentiero delle Aquile, which runs round the cliffs, hills and woods above the village and visits a remote pinnettu at Is Tostoinus.

Start from **Taquisara**, where the railway crosses the main road at almost 800m (2625ft). Follow the road in the direction of Seui. A signpost on the left indicates a route to Nuraghe Serbissi, linking with Walk 32, then further along the road, a tree-shaded picnic site stands to the right and there is a signpost for 'Sentiero delle Aquile'. Head for a liquefied gas store and turn left. Follow a red/white-flashed path above houses on a steep, forested slope.

Turn left at a junction and the path is easier – undulating, but generally climbing, sometimes rocky or stony, and sometimes grassy. It runs in and out of pines and mixed forest. Simply follow this path and climb gradually across steep and rocky slopes, with fine views down the valley. A limestone terrace is followed, and the path swings round a hollow on the rugged hillside. Later, while swinging round a smaller hollow, there is a notice about a cave, **Grotta Cabu de Abba.** Continue along the gentle path then step onto a higher terrace for a while. Drop down stone steps at the head of a rocky gully then climb across a well-grazed, rocky slope thick with asphodels.

141

The path levels out and swings markedly right, with a distant view of the rock tower of Perda Liana. Follow the path across a dip, noticing a nearby zigzag track, and reach a signpost at **Su Segau**, at 995m (3265ft). Walk ahead, gently down a path flanked by stones. The stones run out in a dip, so watch for the trodden path while climbing. The path then regains flanking stones and heads left. Cross a rise and head downhill, watching for red/white flashes as the path goes down steps in a little cleft. The path becomes narrow and rugged, dropping and winding down stone steps, zigzagging down little cliffs. Go through gates to pass through a fenced enclosure containing a large pinnettu at **Is Tostoinus**, at 880m (2885ft).

Turn right on leaving the enclosure, following a rugged track past tall and dense holm oaks. Cross a riverbed and keep right, always following the clearest track at a couple of junctions. Walk up to another junction at **Antepadentes**, at 886m (2907ft). Turn left up a tarmac road and right along a track, which rises onto a broad and grassy area, becoming stone-paved. Undulate in and out of wooded, grassy and bushy areas in a broad valley. A large open area is passed on a gentle ascent to a track junction at **Perdu Isu**, at 965m (3165ft).

View back along the route from the wooded uplands near Nuraghe Perdu Isu

Keep left, or straight ahead, up into woods, passing a **picnic site**. A narrow track winds up to a signpost,

then a right turn is made up a broad and winding path. This climbs among holm oaks, passing charcoal-burning hearths. Turn left at a path junction to follow a winding path, with stone steps, markers and more signposts, through an area of outcrops, massive boulders and stumps of rock. The path splits, with steps to the right leading to an ancient tomb at **Pozzo Sacro**, while left leads to more steps and the ruins of the stone tower **Nuraghe Perdu Isu**. Visit both places before retracing steps back downhill.

The main path is signposted for 'Taquisara' and rises beside a fence for a short way to another path junction. Turn left through a breach and follow stone steps, **Scala de Mesumata**, down through a cleft in a cliff. A winding, zigzag path with more steps drops down a remarkably bouldery slope. Continue down through woods to reach a **picnic site** beside a road. Turn right to follow the road gently downhill. Finally fork left into **Taquisara**, where the road becomes the concrete Via Iliesi into the village.

WALK 34
Perda Liana from Genna Filigi

Distance	3km (from/to Pinningassu) or 10km (2 or 6¼ miles)
Start/finish	Genna Filigi
Alternative start/finish	Pinningassu
Total ascent/descent	125 or 300m (410 or 985ft)
Time	1hr 30min or 4hrs
Map	IGMI 'Serie 50' 531, 'Serie 25' 531 IV
Terrain	Choose either a short, stony path from Pinningassu and back, or a longer walk on roads, tracks and paths, and on open and wooded slopes, sometimes steep. This is a particularly remote area with no facilities.
Refreshment	None
Transport/access	No public transport. Park at either Genna Filigi for the long walk or Pinningassu for the short walk.
Note	Route uses waymarked trail 101

Several Sardinian summits are towers of rock, especially in limestone areas, but Perda Liana is particularly striking. There are two routes described here – the short walk being in the middle of the longer walk. The shorter route is easier and climbs towards the tower to make a circuit around its shoulders. The other offers a longer circuit covering more of the mountain.

There is a road junction and mapboard on a gap at **Genna Filigi**, at 976m (3202ft). Follow the road uphill, signposted for 'Pinningassu', across a slope of arbutus, holm oak and heather. Most of the time, there are views of the rock tower of Perda Liana across a well-wooded valley, as the road rises and falls gently for well over an hour. Fork right along stone-paved road to reach a car park at **Pinningassu**, at 1060m (3480ft). There is another mapboard here, where the short walk, signposted 'Anello di Perda Liana', starts and finishes.

Leave the car park to cross a bridge over the tarmac road. A path continues towards the mountain, up a few stone steps, then straight ahead alongside a fence, up and across a slope of arbutus and heather. Zigzag up more stone steps onto a heathery shoulder, where there is a magnificent view of the rock tower, as well as other high mountains. Reach a signposted path junction and turn right. The path rises and falls on slopes of schist, studded with boulders of limestone fallen from Perda Liana, often washed with quartz pebbles from a bed of conglomerate. Rise again and keep left at two path junctions, the second one bearing a signpost. Keep left to reach a point where paths cross each other.

For the short walk, continue straight ahead to return to the path junction

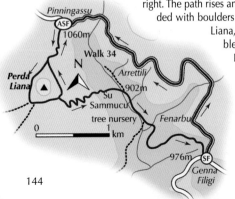

144

The limestone tower, or taccu, of Perda Liana sheds huge boulders onto surrounding slopes

on the shoulder of the mountain and drop back down to Pinningassu. For the long walk, turn right as signposted for 'Fonte Su Sammucu'. A grassy path flanked by stones rises gently, then steep and stony zigzags drop past outcrops of schist, heading in and out of heather and arbutus. The path is plain and obvious, flashed red/white, passing through denser woodland at the bottom. Cross a stream-bed, pass a hut and walk straight down a grassy track past young trees.

Ford a river at a picnic site beneath a huge holm oak at **Su Sammucu**, at 902m (2959ft). Walk along a valley track, which is fenced as it passes a **tree nursery**. Later, keep straight ahead at a junction as signposted, cross a river using a culvert bridge, and climb past arbutus and heather. Keep right at a junction and pass a picnic site before the track joins a road to finish back at **Genna Filigi**.

145

WALK 35

Laconi and Santa Sofia

Distance	19km (12 miles)
Start/finish	Piazza Marconi, Laconi
Total ascent/descent	450m (1475ft)
Time	6hrs
Map	IGMI 'Serie 50' 530, 'Serie 25' 530 III
Terrain	Well-wooded parkland paths, as well as forest tracks and roads, through gentle rolling countryside
Refreshment	Bars and restaurants in Laconi
Transport/access	Regular daily buses serve Laconi from Cagliari, Aritzo and Nuoro
Note	Route uses waymarked trails 261, 262 and 263

Laconi features a fine palace, a ruined castle, the humble home of Sardinia's only saint, Sant' Ignazio, and a church dedicated to his memory. This walk visits a splendid wooded park at the start and finish, and although the walk is long, it runs easily through forest and farmland, seeking features of interest. It is possible to create a longer walk by combining this with Walk 36.

Start in the middle of **Laconi**, below Palazzo Aymerich. Walk up the stone-paved Via Sant' Ignazio and down to the 18th-century saint's birthplace, or Casa Natale. Turn left up Via Don Minzoni, where there is an entrance to Parco Aymerich (or Parco Laconi), but it is better to turn left and right, going through a tunnel under the church to follow Via S Satta and Via Su Acili. Another entrance to **Parco Aymerich** is reached, where there is a mapboard. (The park is open daily from 0800 to 1600.) Follow signs for 'Castello', past a wooden hut beside tall eucalyptus, to reach the ruins of **Castello Aymerich**.

Double back from the castle and turn right to pass the hut, as signposted for 'Pranu Istadi'. Walk uphill

and turn right along a broad path, Su Caminu de Su Marchesu, passing tall trees, mainly holm oaks. Turn sharp left at a signpost, and sharp right along a grassy belvedere overlooking the castle, church and village. Fork left and later pass a viewpoint, walking parallel to a railway. Further along, the path heads downhill, through a little gate onto a track. Turn left for a short, steep climb to a junction at **Pranu Istadi**, where there is a mapboard at 610m (2000ft).

A viewpoint in Parco Aymerich overlooks the castle, church and town of Laconi

Turn left, and the track becomes a road after crossing the **railway**. Turn left at a junction as signposted, and right onto a main road. Turn left up a track signposted for 'Biancone', heading through tall gates into coniferous forest. Climb straight ahead until a clearer track is reached. Turn left down it, passing other tracks to left and right at **Sarcia**. Turn right as signposted along a clear track, climbing to **Funtana Sola**, at 710m (2330ft). Turn right at a signpost and follow a bendy track to a much clearer track at another signpost. Turn right along the main track, not a lesser one running parallel, and pass through a gateway at **Biancone**, where there is a mapboard, around 750m

Also on the left is a track that is part of Walk 36. An extension is possible by following Walk 36 and rejoining Walk 35 at Sa Palla 'e S' Ossiga.

(2460ft). Just to the left an enclosure contains *cervo sardo*, or Sardinian deer. ◀

Follow the clearest track ahead from a complex junction, signposted for 'Sa Palla 'e S' Ossiga'. A **forestry house** lies to the left, followed by a large **pinnettu**. Climb through holm oak woods and pass a notice concerning Sarcidano horses, which live in the forest and might be seen. Also pass a crumbling limekiln. Keep climbing, reaching a slight dip where another track crosses. (Here a detour can be made onto **Gurduxiones** – see Walk 36 for more detail.) Keep straight ahead until the track drops more steeply. Turn right up a lesser track, left at a junction, and down to a junction at **Sa Palla 'e S' Ossiga**, at 825m (2705ft).

Turn right to follow a track signposted for 'Genna 'e Teula'. Soon, there is another signpost on the right, pointing up a broad firebreak. ▶ Follow the track out of the forest and continue along a dirt road through fields, then along a tarmac road. Reach a main road near a Km7 marker, where there is a mapboard and signpost at **Genna 'e Teula**, at 770m (2525ft). (Buses run to and from Laconi along this road.)

This path offers an option to climb to a ruined chapel, Chiesa Santa Sofia, 1.5km (1 mile) there and back.

Cross the road and turn right along an old track running parallel to it. The road rises through a limestone cutting, while the path climbs higher, briefly passing through a holm oak wood. As the road and track run downhill, pass a Km6 marker and fork left where a clear track leaves the road. Keep straight ahead at a junction, gently down a broad, grassy, flowery swathe, flanked by fences and forest. The track undulates gently, runs down through the forest at **Perda Tonara**, out through fields and into holm oak woods. Turn right at a junction, right again along a road through holm oak woods, and right yet again to cross a railway at Casello 22, a rail-side dwelling. ▶

There is an option to turn left here and walk to a monument commemorating four airmen. It is 2km (1½ miles) there and back.

Turn right along the road and later go straight ahead at a junction. The bendy road climbs, with grazing for cattle and sheep down to the left, and rampant lentisc and cistus up to the right. ▶ Walk down the road and turn left as signposted along another track. There is forest to the left and fields to the right, with a junction at **Sa Sucraxia**, at 630m (2065ft). Walk ahead, down a grassy track towards a house, and follow its access track. A mapboard and signpost are reached at a junction at **Pranu Istadi**, at 610m (2000ft). This was passed earlier in the day, so retrace your steps through **Parco Aymerich** to return to **Laconi**.

770m
Genna 'e Teula

On the crest of the road, a track on the left climbs through forest to the Monumento di Sant' Ignazio a Cavallo (a sculpture of the saint on horseback). It is 3km (2 miles) there-and-back.

WALK 36
Funtanamela and Gurduxiones

Distance	9km (5½ miles) or with extension 10km (6 miles)
Start/finish	Funtanamela
Total ascent/descent	125m (410ft)
Time	3hrs
Map	IGMI 'Serie 50' 530, 'Serie 25' 530 III
Terrain	Easy and gently graded forest tracks over low hills
Refreshment	None
Transport/access	No public transport. Funtanamela is at Km74 II on the SS128 road north-west of Laconi, around 700m (2295ft).
Note	Route uses waymarked trails 263 and 264

This short and easy circular walk abounds in interest – featuring waterfalls, an old quarry, extensive forest, a good viewpoint, a big pinnettu, and opportunities to spot Sarcidano horses and Sardinian deer. To create a longer route, walkers based in Laconi could combine it with all or part of Walk 35.

At **Funtanamela** there is a mapboard beside the road and access to a forest picnic site near a waterfall. Walk down the road towards the Km74 sign, turning left up a gentle forest road signposted for 'Sa Palla 'e S'Ossiga'. Go under a **railway** and later turn left up a track, passing a couple of little buildings to reach an old clay quarry at **Cave di Argilla**. Turn left along a track, passing the quarry, heading back into mixed forest. Keep right where the track splits, running level or rising gently past holm oaks and pines. There is a limekiln to the right, just before a junction of tracks at a mapboard at **Sa Palla 'e S' Ossiga**, at 825m (2705ft). ►

Turn right as signposted for 'Biancone' up a narrower, stony track. Watch for more signposts, turning right again along a lesser track. This quickly leads down to a clearer track. Turn left up this, reaching an intersection of tracks where an optional extension is possible to Gurduxiones. To stay on the main route, walk straight ahead.

The route joins Walk 35 here.

Extension to Gurduxiones (1km/½ mile return)

Turn right as signposted for 'Gurduxiones'. A track climbs gently through the forest, swinging left to reach a lookout in a clearing. There are views beyond extensive forests towards the Gennargentu massif. Walk back down the track and turn right to continue along the main route.

Follow the track down past a crumbling limekiln and a notice concerning Sarcidano horses, which live in the forest and might be seen. Pass a large **pinnettu** and a **forest house**, eventually reaching a complex junction of

A vedetta (lookout) on top of Gurduxiones allows views towards the higher mountains of Gennargentu

At this point Walk 35 could be followed in reverse, through a prominent gateway, to Laconi.

tracks at **Biancone**, where there is a mapboard, around 750m (2460ft). Just ahead, an enclosure contains cervo sardo, or Sardinian deer. ◀

Turn right down a track signposted for 'Funtanamela', rising past fenced enclosures and a deer fence. Pass a notice explaining about *aie carbonili*, or charcoal-burning hearths. Walk down to a track junction at a corner of the deer fence and turn right uphill. Pass several charcoal-burning hearths while climbing through holm oak woods. Turn right as signposted to reach another junction, and turn left uphill. The track undulates and passes a lime-kiln, heading downhill with a brief view from a fenced edge. Turn sharp left, down to a twin-track stretch of **railway**, passing a building. Follow the track across the line and down to a road. Turn sharp right to follow the road back to **Funtanamela**. There are tantalising views of multiple cascades in the woods, which might be explored from the picnic site.

WALK 37
Punta La Marmora from S'Arena

Distance	15km (9½ miles) return
Start/finish	Rifugio Sa Crista, S'Arena
Total ascent/descent	350m (1150ft)
Time	5hrs
Map	IGMI 'Serie 50' 516 and 530, 'Serie 25' 516 II and 530 I
Terrain	Clear paths across gentle and rocky slopes onto the highest mountains
Refreshment	Rifugio Sa Crista
Transport/access	S'Arena is 6.5km (4 miles) from a bus route at S' Arcu de Tascussi. By car, head for S' Arcu de Tascussi, between Fonni and Desulo, where five roads meet. Follow the road signposted for 'S'Arena' to Rifugio Sa Crista.
Note	Route uses waymarked trail number 721

Punta La Marmora is the highest point on Sardinia, and despite its remoteness can be climbed relatively easily in fine, clear weather. This is one of three there-and-back walks in the area, the others being Walk 38 and Walk 39. Linking these routes is possible if lifts can be arranged.

At **Rifugio Sa Crista** basic accommodation, food and drink is available, around 1550m (5085ft). The only trees that grow at this altitude are alders in the watercourses,

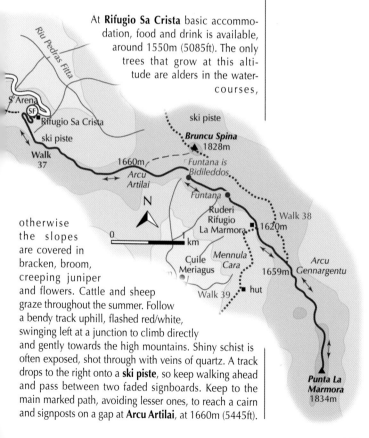

otherwise the slopes are covered in bracken, broom, creeping juniper and flowers. Cattle and sheep graze throughout the summer. Follow a bendy track uphill, flashed red/white, swinging left at a junction to climb directly and gently towards the high mountains. Shiny schist is often exposed, shot through with veins of quartz. A track drops to the right onto a **ski piste**, so keep walking ahead and pass between two faded signboards. Keep to the main marked path, avoiding lesser ones, to reach a cairn and signposts on a gap at **Arcu Artilai**, at 1660m (5445ft).

The path roughly contours across the slope, heading for Arcu Gennargentu and Punta La Marmora

Walk straight ahead along the clearest path across a slope. The schist bedrock is rugged, contorted and broken. Views look down into a valley that can be explored on Walk 40. Pass a spring and follow a rebuilt stretch of path, later reaching **Funtana Is Bidileddos**, at 1660m (5445ft), where there is a picnic site among alders. The path drops, passing gnarled outcrops of schist and stands of alder growing from stream-beds, then goes by tumbled ruins at **Ruderi Rifugio La Marmora**, at 1620m (5315ft), where there is another picnic site. ◀

Walk 39 rises from the right here.

Continue straight ahead and the path climbs gradually to the gap of **Arcu Gennargentu**, at 1659m (5443ft). The signposts and red/white markers finish here, but in clear weather there is no problem continuing onwards. Turn right, not up the rocky crest, but along a trodden, cairned path across a slope covered in granite blocks. Reach a gap and turn left along a final, gently climbing path, again on schist bedrock. The crest of the mountain is knobbly, bearing clumps of thrift, and ends with a rocky outcrop bearing a prominent shiny metal cross. This is the summit of **Punta La Marmora**, the highest point in Sardinia. Either retrace your steps or link with Walk 38 or Walk 39.

Punta La Marmora

Sardinia's highest mountain rises to rises to 1834m (6017ft), and was formerly known as Perda Crapias. It was renamed in honour of Alfonso Ferrero La Marmora, a 19th-century military hero and politician. La Marmora's name crops up among street names in every town and village in Sardinia.

WALK 38
Punta La Marmora from Bruncu Spina

Distance	15km (9½ miles) return
Start/finish	Bruncu Spina ski access road
Total ascent/descent	675m (2215ft)
Time	5hrs
Map	IGMI 'Serie 50' 516 and 530, 'Serie 25' 516 II and 530 I
Terrain	A good track onto a mountain crest, then rugged, with some good paths and some vague paths
Refreshment	None
Transport/access	The start is 8km (5 miles) from a bus route at Donnortei. By car, follow a road south from Fonni, then watch for junctions signposted for 'Monte Spada' and 'Bruncu Spina'. Pass Agriturismo Separadorgi, drive through forest, and note (but don't take) a forest track heading down on the left, Cantiere Forestale. Further along the road, watch for a gateway on the right, and park at a space on the left afterwards.

The approach roads serve ski slopes on Monte Spada and Bruncu Spina. A good track climbs onto Bruncu Spina, then a path can be followed along the mountain crest towards Punta La Marmora. To

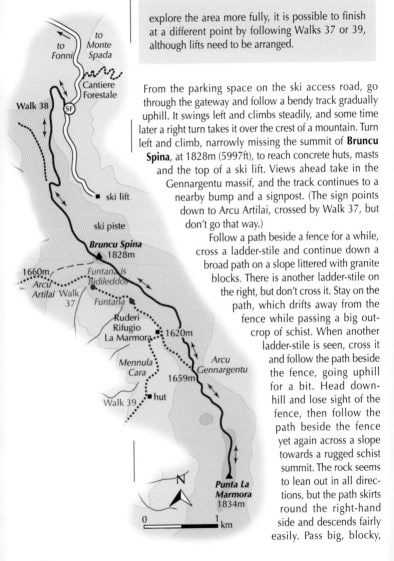

to Fonni
to Monte Spada
Cantiere Forestale
Walk 38
SF
ski lift
ski piste
Bruncu Spina 1828m
1660m
Arcu Artilai Walk 37
Funtana is Bidileddos
Funtana
Ruderi Rifugio La Marmora 1620m
Mennula Cara 1659m
Walk 39 ■ hut
Arcu Gennargentu
N
Punta La Marmora 1834m
0 1 km

explore the area more fully, it is possible to finish at a different point by following Walks 37 or 39, although lifts need to be arranged.

From the parking space on the ski access road, go through the gateway and follow a bendy track gradually uphill. It swings left and climbs steadily, and some time later a right turn takes it over the crest of a mountain. Turn left and climb, narrowly missing the summit of **Bruncu Spina**, at 1828m (5997ft), to reach concrete huts, masts and the top of a ski lift. Views ahead take in the Gennargentu massif, and the track continues to a nearby bump and a signpost. (The sign points down to Arcu Artilai, crossed by Walk 37, but don't go that way.)

Follow a path beside a fence for a while, cross a ladder-stile and continue down a broad path on a slope littered with granite blocks. There is another ladder-stile on the right, but don't cross it. Stay on the path, which drifts away from the fence while passing a big out-crop of schist. When another ladder-stile is seen, cross it and follow the path beside the fence, going uphill for a bit. Head down-hill and lose sight of the fence, then follow the path beside the fence yet again across a slope towards a rugged schist summit. The rock seems to lean out in all directions, but the path skirts round the right-hand side and descends fairly easily. Pass big, blocky,

On a rugged part of the mountain crest, overlooking Arcu Gennargentu, with Punta La Marmora beyond

gnarled outcrops, with fine views ahead, and land on the gap of **Arcu Gennargentu**, at 1659m (5443ft). ▶

There is a signpost here, but no onward signposts or markers. In clear weather there is no problem continuing onwards. Keep straight ahead, not up the rocky crest, but along a trodden, cairned path across a slope covered in granite blocks. Reach a gap and turn left along a final, gently climbing path, again on schist bedrock. The crest of the mountain is knobbly, bearing clumps of thrift, ending with a rocky outcrop bearing a prominent shiny metal cross. This is the summit of **Punta La Marmora**, the highest point in Sardinia, at 1834m (6017ft). This is one of the few places where views are so extensive in clear weather that Sardinia actually looks like an island. Either retrace your steps or descend via Walk 37 or Walk 39.

Walks 37 and 39 also reach this gap.

WALK 39
Punta La Marmora from Cuile Meriagus

Distance	15km (9½ miles) return
Start/finish	Arcu Tuliercu, Cuile Meriagus
Total ascent/descent	660m (2165ft)
Time	5hrs
Map	IGMI 'Serie 50' 516 and 530, 'Serie 25' 516 II and 530 I
Terrain	Good tracks and paths on wooded and rugged slopes
Refreshment	None
Transport/access	No public transport. Access to Cuile Meriagus is possible by driving along the dirt road used on Walk 40 from Arcu Guddetorgiu. Most drivers stop before that and park beside the road at a rock cutting at Arcu Tuliercu, around 1300m (4265ft).

This route is approached via Walk 40, which makes a very long circuit around a fine valley to reach the start of Walk 39 at Arcu Tuliercu. Above the remote summer farm of Cuile Meriagus, the route begins to climb to Punta La Marmora, and links with Walks 37 and 38. Walkers using either of those as return routes need to arrange pick-ups at the end.

Walk down through the cutting at **Arcu Tuliercu**, noticing a pinnettu to the left before fording a river to reach little stone buildings at **Cuile Meriagus**, at 1260m (4135ft). Pass below the buildings and ford two streams at their confluence, where there is a stone-paved ford. Follow the track up a slope planted with saplings, passing a picnic site shaded by a couple of mature trees. The track crosses a crest where there is a stone **hut** and a junction. ◄ Turn left up the track signposted for 'Rifugio La Marmora'. The track climbs past the last of the saplings, and the mountainside has granite boulders scattered across it.

Walk 40 heads downhill from here.

The track passes another stone **hut**, becomes more rugged, and reaches a clump of trees and a well-watered picnic site at **Mennula Cara**, at 1500m (4920ft). Follow a path across a slope to an outcrop of schist, then watch for wooden posts showing the way up to a signpost near the ruins of the former **Rifugio La Marmora**, at 1620m (5315ft). Turn right and refer to Walk 37 to reach **Arcu Gennargentu** and **Punta La Marmora**. Either retrace your steps to **Arcu Tuliercu** or follow Walk 38 to Bruncu Spina or Walk 37 to S'Arena, if pick-ups can be arranged.

A clear track climbs high into the mountains to link with the path from Rifugio Sa Crista

WALK 40
Arcu Guddetorgiu and Girgini

Distance	28km (17½ miles)
Start/finish	Arcu Guddetorgiu
Total ascent/descent	900m (2950ft)
Time	9hrs
Map	IGMI 'Serie 50' 516 and 530, 'Serie 25' 516 II and 530 I
Terrain	Mostly roads and tracks with gentle gradients, but also some rugged paths across steep slopes. Lower parts are wooded, especially towards the end.
Refreshment	None
Transport/access	Arcu Guddetorgiu is 6.5km (4 miles) from bus routes at Desulo and S' Arcu de Tascussi
Note	Route uses waymarked trails 700, 722 and 723

This is a long route around a remote valley among Sardinia's highest mountains. However, most of the distance is along quiet roads and tracks, and if lifts can be arranged along these, it is possible to shorten the route considerably and concentrate on the rugged mountainside paths in the middle.

Arcu Guddetorgiu is a remote crossroads, around 1125m (3690ft), on a high road between Aritzo and Desulo. Start by walking down the road signposted for 'Agriturismo Girgini', but turn left at a bend where another road is signposted for 'Cuile Meriagus'. The road climbs gently past holm oaks and heather, becoming a dirt road as it crosses a river, **Riu Istadda**. Holm oaks give way to deciduous oaks as the road rises and turns round a corner at **Arcu Istadda**, with fine views of high mountains ahead. Descend and cross a stream, climb and keep right at a fork, then descend again. The slopes are dotted with stout oaks that have suffered considerable storm damage, and there are also newly planted trees. The track crosses **Riu Is Luas** at a paved ford, then becomes very bendy as it

climbs. Other
streams run
through culverts.

A track junc-
tion is reached on a hair-
pin bend, where **Funtana 'e Piraone** lies
to the right, so keep left to continue climbing. There is a
short-cut straight uphill if desired; otherwise stay on the
track and turn another hairpin bend near a small hut. Turn
a corner at **Arcu Tuliercu**, around 1300m (4265ft) (start of
Walk 39), and go down through a rock cutting. Notice
a pinnettu to the left before fording a river to reach little
stone buildings at **Cuile Meriagus**, at 1260m (4135ft).

Pass below the buildings and ford two streams at
their confluence, where there is a stone-paved ford.
Follow the track up a slope planted with saplings, passing

Walk 39 turns left here.

a picnic site shaded by a couple of mature trees. The track crosses a crest where there is a stone **hut** and a junction. ◄ Keep ahead downhill then rise to another stone **hut**. Just above it, fork right (as flashed red/white) and level out across a slope of impressive granite boulder scree. Reach a junction near **Sa Minna** and keep straight ahead as signposted for 'Girgini', down towards a wood. The track ends, so drop downhill and cross a stream.

Zigzag uphill past low clumps of juniper and a few little yew trees. The path later levels out, with fine views of the valley and surrounding mountains, dipping in and out of a stream-bed where there are trees. Roughly contour across a slope of low, thorny scrub and pass **Funtana 'e Furau**, at 1395m (4575ft), where there are more trees. The path rises and falls, and is rocky in places on the slopes of Bruncu Furau, but generally is easy to follow to **Arcu i Montes**, at 1380m (4530ft). Descend easily above a slope of deciduous oaks, and the path seems to vanish on stone-strewn turf at **Arcu Su Litterau**, at 1335m (4380ft).

A long and winding track offers easy and rapid walking most of the way round the valley

The path actually turns left and quickly becomes obvious as it drops across a slope of granite and heather. Pass planted holm oaks and turn right down a track, back onto a heather slope. Bend left at a signpost, where

a right turn leads only to the nearby **Funtana Lettu Piccinnu**. Simply walk straight down a track, which later winds through a limestone area covered in stout holm oaks. Note the limestone towers, or *tacchi*, protruding from wooded hills, and reach a broad track and picnic site at **Sa Sedda 'e S'Ena**, at 1015m (3330ft). ▶

A signposted detour left along the track allows a visit to a rock tower at Genna Eragas. The distance there and back is 4.5km (2¾ miles).

Turn right as signposted for 'Girgini', following the track round a valley, above a **farm** where there are pigs, cattle and goats. Reach a junction on a gentle, grassy gap at **Su Pranu 'e Girgini**, at 1080m (3545ft). Turn left and soon reach another junction. ▶ Turn right round a bend and head down through holm oak woods, past a building. Later, cross a concrete bridge and walk down to a tarmac road-end and bridge at **Bau 'e Jacca**, at 925m (3035ft).

Walking straight ahead leads to a large shelter and good views.

There are no more signposts or markers, but all that remains is to walk up the bendy road on slopes of holm oak and heather. There are glimpses of farms, and hairpin bends pass **Agriturismo Girgini**. The road finally rises from woods to return to the road junction at **Arcu Guddetorgiu**.

WALK 41
Monte Spada from Genna Luddurreo

Distance	6.5km (4 miles)
Start/finish	Genna Luddurreo
Total ascent/descent	350m (1150ft)
Time	2hrs 30min
Map	IGMI 'Serie 50' 516, 'Serie 25' 516 II
Terrain	A clear track to the summit, followed by a rugged descent. Tracks and rugged, wooded paths around the slopes of the mountain.
Refreshment	A bar/restaurant is passed on the approach road
Transport/access	Genna Luddurreo is 5km (3 miles) from a bus route at Donnortei, near Fonni. By car from Fonni, take the road signposted for 'Monte Spada', then turn right at a bar/restaurant as if heading for Bruncu Spina. There is a parking space on a broad gap at Genna Luddurreo.

Monte Spada's domed form allows it to stand out in distant views. The northern slopes catch enough snow in winter to support a brief ski season. The southern side boasts a clear path, while other paths and tracks can be linked to form a short circular walk round the mountain.

From **Genna Luddurreo**, over 1350m (4430ft), a plain and obvious track climbs straight up a rounded crest, following a fence all the way to the summit of **Monte Spada**, at 1594m (5230ft). There are two crosses – a small rusty one and a large blue one. Views are extensive, stretching from the mountains of Gennargentu to Ogliastra.

Monte Spada is easily climbed from the gentle gap of Genna Luddurreo

From here continue over the mountain by following the fence, unless you prefer to take the easiest descent

by simply to retrace your steps from the summit. A ditch was cut to lay an electricity cable to light the summit cross, so walk on the rubble beside it to avoid thorny scrub on the slope. Head down to a junction of fences and turn left, then walk down to a forest and turn left again. Cross the forest fence to the derelict **Sporting Club** Monte Spada, around 1300m (4265ft). This is at the end of a tarmac road, and here follow a broad track onwards past a **ski piste**. Later, the track turns right uphill, then left through locked gates, where there is a gap for walkers to pass.

The track winds down a steep slope of oaks, then climbs gradually past a couple of springs, with views of the valley of Riu Govossai from time to time. Walk up through gates, then down to a **building**. There are two tracks, both grassy, but keep right and climb past a water tank, noting heather among the trees. Further uphill the track forks, so keep right again, climbing awkwardly up and across a slope of oaks and stones. The path undulates and passes a spring emerging from a pipe, then becomes vague as it approaches a fence. Turn right to follow the fence up from the woods and across a scrubby slope. Cross the fence at a corner and walk down to a track through low scrub. Turn right to follow the track back to the broad gap and road at **Genna Luddurreo**.

WALK 42
Tonara and Punta Muggianeddu

Distance	15km or (to S' Arcu de Tascussi) 13.5km (9½ or 8½ miles)
Start/finish	Church of San Antonio, Tonara
Alternative finish	S' Arcu de Tascussi
Total ascent/descent	700m (2295ft)
Time	5hrs
Map	IGMI 'Serie 50' 516, 'Serie 25' 516 II and III
Terrain	Clear roads and forest tracks, with paths used on higher slopes
Refreshment	Plenty of choice in Tonara; bar at S' Arcu de Tascussi
Transport/access	Regular daily buses serve Tonara from Fonni, Desulo and Sorgono, with links to Nuoro
Note	Route uses waymarked trails 501 and 502

Tonara is a fine mountain village, specialising in the production of *torrone* (nougat) and cow-bells. Punta Muggianeddu stands high above, surrounded by forests, but approachable using convoluted tracks and paths. The walk can be extended to finish at S' Arcu de Tascussi. This option is a little shorter than the main route, but more difficult underfoot.

Start in the centre of **Tonara**, around 850m (2790ft), at the church of San Antonio. (Tonara has a full range of services.) Follow a road uphill, switching to a short flight of stone steps to short-cut a bend. Cross the Via Roma and walk up the stone-paved Via San Antonio. Turn left up the stone-paved Via Mazzini. Turn left up a narrow tarmac road and bend right (signposted 'Camping') to reach a mapboard just before a **youth hostel**.

Follow a bendy road up past the last houses, following a trail flashed red/white, into woods of oak and chestnut. Go through gates and later reach a signposted

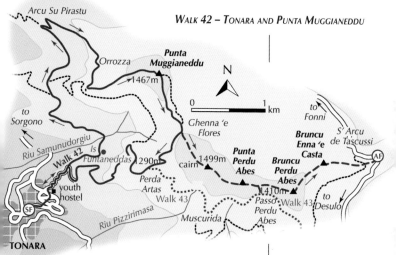

junction. Turn left along a track, and note that the return route comes back down the road. When three tracks split apart, keep to the middle one, which rises through woods and passes a spring at **Is Funtaneddas**. The track crosses a crest and drops past Sa Funtana de S'Abe, then crosses a stream, **Riu Samunudorgiu**.

As the track undulates onwards pines become dominant, and there are glimpses of Tonara. Emerge from tall forest onto a slope of bushy heather. Keep straight ahead up the main track, which has cypresses alongside. Keep right uphill at a junction and climb gently to another junction, turning left downhill as signposted. Pass dense holm oaks, with a few chestnuts, then rise gently and keep right at a fork, staying on the main track. Turn sharp right uphill at a signposted junction at **Arcu Su Pirastu**, and the track bends left, then right, to reach a higher junction. Keep right (in effect straight ahead), climbing across a slope of bushy heather into mixed forest. Level out among holm oaks at a spring at **Orrozza**. The track continues easily through pine forest with cypresses alongside.

Turn left up a lesser track, signposted for 'Punta Muggianeddu', where the pines thin out and the slope is covered in flaky schist and quartz. Go through a gateway

167

in a fence and follow a drystone wall and fence uphill. Pines give way to heather and thorny scrub, then after going through a gate in an adjoining fence, continue on short turf. Go through a gateway on the right to reach the summit of **Punta Muggianeddu**, at 1467m (4813ft), where there is a mast and a lookout. Views along the broad crest might tempt some walkers to consider heading for the heart of the Gennargentu massif.

There are two ways down from the summit – either of which can be taken. The most obvious and easy is the access road from the mast. The other route is marked by a signpost, revealing a vague path down beside a drystone wall. Both the track and path lead downhill, then climb to a gap, gateway and signpost at **Ghenna 'e Flores**, around 1400m (4595ft). (There is the option here to follow the mountain crest to S' Arcu de Tascussi, described below.)

Walk down the forest track as signposted to 'Tonara'. This continues along a bendy road, which is simply followed downhill, avoiding tracks to right and left. The road passes the signposted junction seen earlier in the day, and heads down through gates to reach the campsite and **youth hostel**. Continue down into **Tonara** to finish.

Extension to S' Arcu de Tascussi (3.75km/2¼ miles)

◀ Climb and squeeze between a wall/fence and a pine plantation. The slope is variously rocky, stony

Arrange to be collected at the finish, or time your arrival to link with a bus.

The church of San Gabriele in Tonara, rebuilt in the 20th century, but standing on an older foundation

or covered in short turf above the forest. Pass a summit where a tall, columnar **cairn** stands to the left, at 1499m (4918ft). Keep to the ridge and its wall/fence, side-stepping rocks where necessary. Drop to a gap and climb the other side onto **Punta Perdu Abes**. Drop down steep and rocky slopes to a forested gap. ▶

> There is a way down to the right, linking with Walk 43, at Passo Perdu Abes.

Climb from the forested gap onto the summit of **Bruncu Perdu Abes**, and follow the wall/fence down the other side. The ridge is very rocky, but walkable. Cross the next gap and climb a short way onto the next summit, **Bruncu Enna 'e Casta**, on short grass strewn with stones. Bear right on top, leaving the wall/fence to pick a way down the least vegetated part of the crest. There are vague paths among low rocks and scrub. Pass a series of statues and crosses, stepping over a track to reach a road junction at **S' Arcu de Tascussi**, around 1250m (4100ft). ▶

> There is a bar here, if you have a long time to wait for a bus or lift.

WALK 43
Bauerì, Passo Perdu Abes and Tonara

Distance	15km (9½ miles)
Start	Km7 at Bauerì
Finish	Church of San Antonio, Tonara
Total ascent	700m (2295ft)
Total descent	550m (1805ft)
Time	5hrs
Map	IGMI 'Serie 50' 516, 'Serie 25' 516 II and III
Terrain	Good forest tracks and hillside tracks, climbing and falling gradually
Refreshment	Plenty of choice in Tonara
Transport/access	Regular daily buses serve Tonara and Bauerì from Fonni, Desulo and Sorgono, with links to Nuoro. If you catch a bus from Tonara to Bauerì, at the end of the day forest and hill tracks can be followed to return to Tonara from Bauerì.
Note	Route uses waymarked trail 502

Easy forest and hill tracks climb high into the mountains, sometimes passing good viewpoints. At its highest point this walk can be linked with Walk 42, and earlier there is the option to reach a remote road junction at S' Arcu de Tascussi.

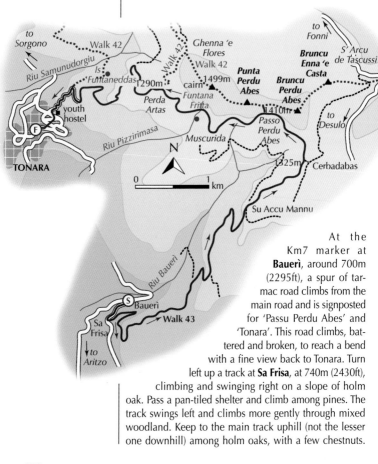

At the Km7 marker at **Bauerì**, around 700m (2295ft), a spur of tarmac road climbs from the main road and is signposted for 'Passu Perdu Abes' and 'Tonara'. This road climbs, battered and broken, to reach a bend with a fine view back to Tonara. Turn left up a track at **Sa Frisa**, at 740m (2430ft), climbing and swinging right on a slope of holm oak. Pass a pan-tiled shelter and climb among pines. The track swings left and climbs more gently through mixed woodland. Keep to the main track uphill (not the lesser one downhill) among holm oaks, with a few chestnuts.

Keep right where another track heads down to the left, and climb more steeply round right and left bends. The surface is stony in places, with heather scrub alongside. Keep climbing ahead through dense woods, straight through a skewed intersection of tracks.

A fine track climbs gradually across forested slopes high above Riu Bauerì

The track later bends right and the woods are quite mixed. Bend left later, climbing as the woods give way to heather scrub. Reach another skewed intersection of tracks, where there is a signpost, at **Su Accu Mannu**. Keep straight ahead up the rugged track, across a slope of heather to another junction and signpost near **Cerbadabas**, at 1325m (4345ft). Again keep straight ahead up the rugged track. Turning right reveals a view of the village of Desulo and mountains beyond. ▶ The track reaches a gateway in a straggly fence at **Passo Perdu Abes**, at 1410m (4625ft). Views stretch to the highest mountain in Sardinia, Punta La Marmora. ▶

A track can be followed from here to S' Arcu de Tascussi.

Turning right here reveals a path climbing to link with Walk 42.

Start following the track downhill into pine forest, levelling out and even rising gently, with occasional views of the mountains. Keep straight ahead at a junction at **Muscurida**, avoiding a left turn. At the next junction, however, fork left downhill and later pass **Funtana Fritta**. Further down, a sharp left turn leads to a picnic

At this point the route links with Walk 42 from Punta Muggianeddu.

site at Usolí, but keep straight ahead to reach a junction at **Perda Artas**, at 1290m (4230ft). ◄ Follow the track and a bendy road downhill, avoiding tracks to right and left. The road passes a signposted junction, heading down through gates to reach a campsite and **youth hostel**.

Either follow the tarmac road down into the village or seek out the quieter stone-paved streets of Via Mazzini and Via San Antonio, and a short-cut down a flight of steps from the Via Roma. Finish in the centre of **Tonara** at the church of San Antonio, around 850m (2790ft).

WALK 44
Meana Sardo to Aritzo

Distance	31km (19¼ miles) or, with the summit of Meseddu de Texile, 32km (19¾ miles)
Start	Meana Sardo
Finish	Aritzo
Total ascent	1050m (3525ft)
Total descent	900m (2950ft)
Time	10hrs
Map	IGMI 'Serie 50' 530, 'Serie 25' 530 I and IV
Terrain	Mostly along clear forest tracks and linking paths, as well as roads and a railway line
Refreshment	Bars and restaurants in Meana Sardo and Aritzo
Transport/access	Daily buses serve Meana Sardo and Aritzo from Cagliari and Nuoro
Note	Route uses waymarked trail 521

Meana Sardo and Aritzo are typical Sardinian mountain villages, but lie distant from each other by road. However, there is a waymarked walking trail linking them together, traversing forested mountains and valleys. Towards the end, a fine rocky summit, or taccu, called Meseddu de Texile can be climbed.

From **Meana Sardo**, around 600m (1970ft), follow the main road uphill from the village to the Km86 marker, where there is a roadside funtana. (Meana Sardo has a good range of services and a little accommodation.) A path can be followed across the wooded slope parallel to the road, but only for a short way, then the road is followed onwards. Don't cross a bridge over a railway, but turn left down a track signposted for 'Bruncu Sant' Elias' and go through a **tunnel** under the railway. Don't follow the track climbing steeply left, but stay low in the valley and follow a grassy track beside a stream, fording it once.

Turn right up a steep track. Keep right at a fork and climb steeply, flanked by bushy heather, past another track, to reach a clearer track and signposts at a higher level. Cross this track and continue up another, climbing into mixed forest, gaining a clear view of Bruncu Sant' Elias. Turn left along a broad path, which looks gently graded, but later climbs steeply through dense holm oak, reaching a picnic site and a hut at **Su Accili de S'Ilixedda**, at 880m (2885ft).

Looking down forested slopes to see Meana Sardo spread either side of a small hill

Walk past the hut, turn left along a track and pass a spring. Turn right up a few steps to follow a path parallel to a woodland track, and walk through a stone

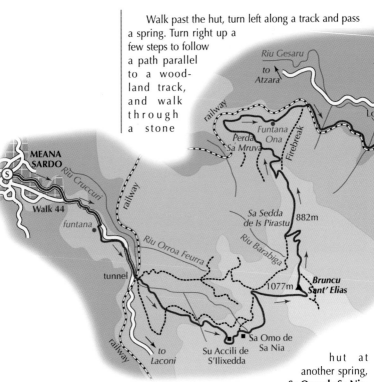

hut at another spring, **Sa Omo de Sa Nia**.

Continue along the track, round a bend, then go up steps to climb to a higher track. Turn left down to a junction and keep straight ahead, following a path parallel to a track. Turn right up a broad, steep firebreak to the top of the forest. Cross a stile and follow a winding path up a scrubby, rocky slope to a signpost near the summit of **Bruncu Sant' Elias**, at 1077m (3535ft). Pass a tall mast to sample the view.

Cross a ladder-stile and go down a red/white-flashed path on a scrubby slope to arrive on a clear track. Turn left along it and go down through a gate, winding into pine forest. Turn right at a junction and walk down the

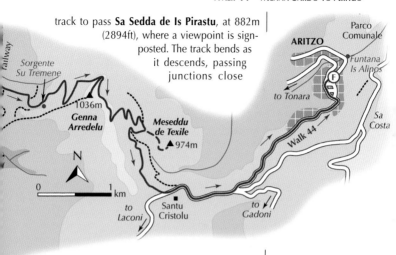

track to pass **Sa Sedda de Is Pirastu**, at 882m (2894ft), where a viewpoint is signposted. The track bends as it descends, passing junctions close together, as well as a tin hut. Turn right, and right again, at the next two junctions and roughly contour through mixed woods. When the track drops, turn right up another track, which rises and falls. Pass a concrete water store at **Funtana Ona** and later turn left down a firebreak.

Drop down to a **railway** and turn right to follow it as signposted. The line is quite bendy, crossing a four-arched bridge, passing a building and running through two cuttings. Cross a five-arched bridge, go through more cuttings, and cross another five-arched bridge. Pass another building and cross an eight-arched bridge. Go through more cuttings and cross two more five-arched bridges. The engineering of this mountain railway is incredible, but trains use it only in high summer. ▸

Leave the line as signposted, cross a ladder-stile and walk up a short, grassy, zigzag path. Turn left up a grassy track, above ruined buildings beside the railway. Turn left along another grassy track at **Lorossa**, at 600m (1970ft), among cork oak trees. There is a slight descent, then climb round wooded slopes to reach a junction and turn left as signposted for 'Meseddu de Texile'. Climb through

If you do follow this line in summer, be aware of the timetable, and be ready to move to a safe place if a train comes along.

175

low, mixed woods and bushy scrub, with one stretch on concrete.

Keep right at a junction and left at another, mostly among holm oaks. There are more concrete stretches, with arbutus alongside, past **Sorgente Su Tremene**. Keep climbing the bendy track, and pines are dotted about the mountain scrub towards the top. A signpost points right for a short there-and-back walk to the top of **Genna Arredelu**, at 1036m (3399ft), which offers a view down to Aritzo.

The track rises and falls beside a drystone wall and reaches a junction on a gentle gap. Turn left down the bendy track on a slope of heather, arbutus and pines. Go straight ahead at a junction, and straight ahead at the next junction too. Soon afterwards, at another junction, turning left allows a nearby rocky summit to be visited. (Turning right allows a short-cut to a main road.)

Ascent of Meseddu de Texile (1km/½ mile return)

To visit the summit, follow a track up a crest of pines, emerging from the forest beneath overhanging cliffs. Keep to the right, and a breach can be exploited, leading onto Meseddu de Texile, at 974m (3196ft). Forestry maps show a walking route from here down to Aritzo, but this is completely overgrown and cannot be recommended. Instead, retrace your steps to the track junction.

From the junction follow the track to the main road at **Santu Cristolu**. There are buses, but if none is due, then turn left down the road. This leads easily down across wooded slopes and, by keeping left at a junction, eventually reaches **Aritzo**, around 800m (2625ft).

WALK 45
Aritzo and Geratzia

Distance	10km (6¼ miles)
Start/finish	Church in Aritzo
Total ascent/descent	450m (1475ft)
Time	3hrs
Map	IGMI 'Serie 50' 530, 'Serie 25' 530 I
Terrain	Rugged hillside paths, good woodland tracks and mountain roads
Refreshment	Bars and restaurants in Aritzo
Transport/access	Occasional daily buses serve Aritzo from Cagliari, Laconi, Tonara, Fonni and Nuoro

Anyone finding themselves in the lovely mountain village of Aritzo with a few hours to spare can enjoy a fine short walk from the centre, taking in a lovely waterfall, fine viewpoint and some remarkably stout chestnut trees. A quiet mountain road and steep tracks return to Aritzo.

Start at the church in the centre of **Aritzo**, around 800m (2625ft), and walk down the main road, Corso Umberto, where there is a good range of services. Turn right up Via Is Alinos, and the steep concrete road levels out and is stone-paved to **Funtana Is Alinos**. At this point there is a waterfall and access to the **Parco**

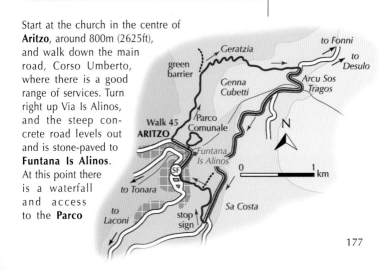

177

Comunale, but bear in mind that any explorations must return to this point to continue the walk.

Parco Comunale

To explore the rugged park, cross a ladder-stile beside gates and walk up a mock-paved path, which gives way to a gravel path. Keep right as marked 'Sentieri', then note that other right turns require steps to be retraced afterwards. So, the simplest way is to keep left and keep zigzagging up the fenced path. This passes a sign, 'Castagneto', where there are chestnuts, and leads to Punta Ferula for a fine view over Aritzo and its surrounding mountains. Follow the path as it winds back downhill to Funtana Is Alinos.

The stout trunks of ancient chestnut trees at Geratzia catch the winter snow

Turn right to follow a concrete road past houses, then turn right again along a concrete track signposted for 'Geratzia'. Only a few parts of the track are concrete, and the rest is stony, winding and undulating. Stay on it, and avoid all spurs leading right and left to properties alongside. Eventually, pass a small, solitary white house,

which lies to the right, and reach a point where a track climbs right, between green posts and a **green barrier**. Immediately fork left up a clear track, climbing and winding past chestnuts with a view of Aritzo and Belvi. Pass another barrier gate and turn right at a junction. Climb, with more chestnuts on the right, then chestnuts on both sides at **Geratzia**. Continue through mixed woods, then keep right on leaving the woods.

Follow a clear track up a slope of dense heather, with views of Tonara and Desulo. All spurs off this track are gated and private, so keep climbing to reach a road, around 1100m (3610ft). Turn right to walk down it, round a bend at **Arcu Sos Tragos**, with a wooded valley below. Later, there are chestnuts on either side, and later still there are good views of Aritzo. Continue down until a road on the left is signposted with many destinations, while further down a **'Stop' sign** stands on the right. A clear track drops from here, becoming concrete. It is very steep as it becomes the Via Scala Valeri, which leads into the top part of **Aritzo**. Turn left down Via Moros, right down Via La Marmora, and left down Via Arangino to return to the church.

WALK 46
Teti and S'Urbale

Distance	8km (5 miles)
Start/finish	Museo Archeologico, Teti
Total ascent/descent	200m (655ft)
Time	2hrs 30min
Map	IGMI 'Serie 50' 516, 'Serie 25' 516 III and IV
Terrain	The ascent is by road, and the descent uses clear tracks, mostly on wooded slopes
Refreshment	Bars in Teti
Transport/access	Buses serve Teti from Nuoro, with occasional links to Sorgono, except Sundays
Note	Route uses waymarked trail 515A

Teti clings to a steep slope and enjoys splendid valley views. The surrounding countryside is rich in archaeological remains, and there is a dedicated archaeological museum in Teti. Every street nameplate and house number throughout the village features a Bronze Age motif. This route follows easy tracks to explore the countryside.

Start at the bottom end of the village of **Teti**, around 700m (2295ft), where the Museo Archeologico is located on Via Roma. If it is closed, make a note to visit another time. Return to the main road and choose one of two ways up through the village. The main road is Corso Italia, climbing from the Km23 marker past the church of Santa Maria delle Nevi, bending right and left as it gains height. A more direct ascent from the Km23 marker is available using Via E Berlinguer, turning left when the main road is joined. Either way, follow the main road onwards and upwards, passing an attractive funtana at **Su Cantaru**. Reach a crossroads on a gap at **Istei**, at 847m (2779ft), where the route turns right along a track.

Before following the track, climb up steps from the crossroads, following a broad and grassy track that later weaves through the nuraghic village of **S'Urbale**. Inter-linked hut circles sprawl across a crest bearing cork oaks, holm oaks and deciduous oaks. When the path peters out, turn round and walk back down to the crossroads and follow the track, as signposted for 'Nuraghe Alinedu'. When a junction of tracks is reached, head down to the right and continue straight ahead past

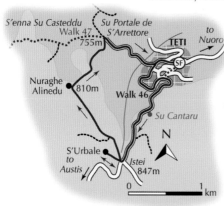

a farm access track and fields. The track suddenly turns right, and although access is barred by a fence **Nuraghe Alinedu** is easily seen, at 810m (2660ft).

Follow the track down and up, passing a big granite outcrop and dropping again. There are big deciduous oaks in fields, but also conifers down on the right, with Teti in view. A signposted, granite-paved junction is reached at **Su Portale de S'Arrettore**, at 755m (2475ft). ▶

Turn right and walk down the road, which drops more steeply later, passing lots of deciduous oaks before crossing a bridge. Climb steeply to a junction with Via Boccaccio and turn left to follow it to the Corso Italia in **Teti**. Turn left to follow this down through the village. (If a short-cut to the museum is needed, pass the Municipio, then fork left down the narrower Via Dante. Turn right at the bottom along Via Caserma, then immediately left along Via Roma.)

Several fine hut circles can be inspected at the nuraghic village of S'Urbale

There is an option here to turn left and follow Walk 47.

WALK 47
Teti and Craru Eridunele

Distance	12km (7½ miles)
Start/finish	Teti
Total ascent/descent	250m (820ft)
Time	4hrs
Map	IGMI 'Serie 50' 516, 'Serie 25' 516 III and IV
Terrain	Minor roads, farm tracks and forest tracks, mostly on gentle slopes
Refreshment	Bars in Teti
Transport/access	Buses serve Teti from Nuoro, with occasional links to Sorgono, except Sundays
Note	Route uses waymarked trail 515B

A fine track can be followed westwards from the village of Teti across rolling hillsides to a forest. Rather surprisingly, since the area seems remote, there is a fitness trail in the forest. Tracks are followed in a loop before the return route retraces steps to Teti.

Start at the bottom end of the village of **Teti**, around 700m (2295ft). Follow the main road, Corso Italia, uphill from the Km23 marker, past the church of Santa Maria delle Nevi. Pass the Municipio and veer right along Via Boccaccio, leaving the village and turning right down to a bridge. Follow the road uphill, steeply at first, then more gently, past lots of deciduous oaks. Reach a granite-paved junction of tracks at **Su Portale de S'Arrettore**, at 755m (2475ft). ◀

There is a junction here with Walk 46.

Walk straight up a granite-paved track signposted 'Craru Eridunele'. Neat stone slabs give way to more uneven paving as the track crosses a hill and passes fields. Drop into a dip, then climb along a more rugged track over another hillside and note the bouldery clearance heaps in a field to the right. The track descends gently across

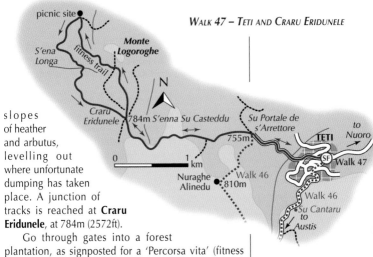

slopes of heather and arbutus, levelling out where unfortunate dumping has taken place. A junction of tracks is reached at **Craru Eridunele**, at 784m (2572ft).

Go through gates into a forest plantation, as signposted for a 'Percorsa vita' (fitness trail). Walk gently up and down the track, passing fitness equipment, and continue as signposted through a track intersection. The forest becomes more mixed, notably with pale green cypresses alongside, and there are views as the track runs downhill, along with more natural

A remarkable granite-paved road rises and falls through gently rolling countryside

183

woodland cover, with granite tors. The track reaches gates at a junction with a clearer track, around 725m (2380ft), and more gates lead into a pine-shaded **picnic site**, if required.

Turn left along the clear track, undulating gently, but generally climbing. Pass intriguing granite outcrops and a huge boulder, and later climb between two large fields to return to the track junction at **Craru Eridunele**. Turn right to pick up the track leading back to **Teti**.

WALK 48
Sorradile and Monte Cresia

Distance	14km (8½ miles)
Start/finish	Sorradile
Total ascent/descent	400m (1310ft)
Time	4hrs
Map	IGMI 'Serie 50' 515, 'Serie 25' 515 I
Terrain	Roads, tracks and occasional paths on wooded and farmed slopes
Refreshment	Bars in Sorradile
Transport/access	Regular daily buses serve Sorradile from Abbasanta and occasionally from Fonni, Desulo and Sorgono
Note	Route uses waymarked trail 513

The countryside around Sorradile and Bidoni is rich in archaeological sites and historic buildings, ranging from *domus de janas* (rock tombs) to *novenario* (country chapels). Monte Cresia makes a fine viewpoint, and, after a winding descent, the route brushes along the shore of Lago Omodeo.

Start at a road bend at the bottom end of **Sorradile**, around 300m (985ft). Follow a narrow road signposted as a walking route to Monte Simeone, climbing steeply, with views of the village and the huge reservoir of Lago Omodeo. Reach a road junction and turn right to climb further. Cross a rise and head down round a bend. Rise gently, then drop steeply to a junction and a stand of eucalyptus trees.

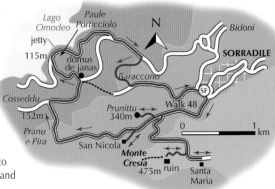

Turn left, bearing in mind that you return here later. The road climbs and bends sharp left, then climbs to a junction and a signpost. First, go straight ahead, over a rise, and visit a lovely 12th-century chapel, **Novenario Santa Maria**, or Santuario Santa Maria di Turrana. Return to the junction and climb a broken concrete road onto **Monte Cresia**, where there is a ruined

The Novenario San Nicola is one of several country churches scattered across this region

church and a lookout tower, around 475m (1560ft). There is a fine view of the reservoir, Sorradile, Abbasanta and Sedilo. Retrace your steps back to the road to the junction with the eucalyptus trees alongside.

Walk down the road until a 'Domus de Janas' signpost and mapboard are seen on the right at **Prunittu**, at 340m (1115ft). A vague path heads down into a rocky valley, where there is a splendid necropolis. The more you look, the more square-cut entrances are seen, leading into elaborate rock tombs. Explore the site, then return to the road and continue to a signposted junction with another road. Turn left to walk up to a 17th-century chapel, **Novenario San Nicola**, or Santuario San Nicola. Return to the road junction or simply short-cut downhill when an opportunity is spotted.

The road descends gently, then steeply, rising and falling before reaching a junction with a main road at **Cosseddu**, at 152m (499ft). Turn right to follow the road across a bridge and round a bend. Fork left along a minor road next to the little hill of Monte Simeone, at 158m (518ft), where there is a splendid domus de janas. The minor road rises and falls to a junction at **Paule Porticciolo**, at 115m (380ft), beside the huge reservoir of **Lago Omodeo**.

Turn right and follow the road back up to the main road. Turn left up the main road, then right up a steep concrete track. The gradient eases and two pairs of locked gates are reached at **Baraccono**. In between them is a narrow, stony path flanked by bushes and brambles, almost like a cobbly stream-bed. Follow it uphill, squeezing past the undergrowth for a few minutes, to emerge on a road. Turn left and follow the road uphill, past a cemetery, climbing steeply back to the road junction where the walk started, at the bottom end of **Sorradile**. It is worth going into the village, where there are bars and the 15th-century church of San Sebastiano.

WALK 49
Sedilo to Ponte Fiume Taloro

Distance	16km (10 miles)
Start	Sedilo
Finish	Ponte Fiume Taloro
Total ascent	275m (900ft)
Total descent	400m (1310ft)
Time	5hrs
Map	IGMI 'Serie 50' 515, 'Serie 25' 515 I
Terrain	Mostly roads at first, then farm and forest tracks with one rugged ascent above Litigheddu
Refreshment	Bars in Sedilo
Transport/access	Regular daily buses serve Sedilo from Abbasanta and Nuoro. Pick-up is required from the finish point, Ponte Fiume Taloro. Alternatively, the nearest bus service is 6km (3¾ miles) away at Bidoni.
Note	Route uses waymarked trail 611

The first half of this linear walk is along an old by-pass road east of Sedilo. The second half is mostly along good tracks, running over a broad crest, passing farms and forests, and descending to Ponte Fiume Taloro.

Start in the centre of **Sedilo**, around 275m (900ft), and follow Corso Eleonora out of town in the direction of Nuoro. The road becomes Viale Martiri della Libertà on the edge of town. When a statue of San Constantino Magno on horseback is reached, turn right down another road. Pass a stone-cross monument and continue down a dirt road to an imposing stone archway. It is worth visiting the **Chiesa San Constantino**, at 223m (732ft), whose interior is adorned with offerings, notably pictures and silver hearts.

A stone monument overlooks Lago Omodeo above the Chiesa San Constantino

Follow the dirt road onwards and it becomes tarmac again, crossing a bridge over an **old by-pass road**. Follow the road away from Sedilo, as signposted for 'Monte Busurtei'. The road runs gently down and round a bend, and there is a signpost on the right. At this point, it is possible to climb nearby Monte Busurtei and visit the ruins of **Nuraghe Busurtei** on its summit, but it is best to regard this as optional. The path onto and down from the hill is rugged and overgrown, while the nuraghe is hidden by bushes. However, there are a few red/white markers indicating the path, but care is needed to spot them. (The loop is 2km (1¼ miles) in length and takes a frustrating hour to complete.)

The old by-pass road goes under a bridge and runs roughly parallel to the **Fiume Tirso**, following it upstream through a valley. The road becomes a track and runs underneath a main road bridge. If the water in the river is low, then it is possible to ford it at **Goado Pedra Lada** and come back underneath the bridge. If the water is high, then don't go under the bridge, but cross the bridge with great care and then drop down to the riverside, following a track downstream. Another signposted junction is reached at **Litigheddu**, at 134m (440ft). Turn left here to follow another track uphill.

The grassy, pebbly track climbs past fields bounded by bouldery walls, passing **Funtana Litigheddu**. The track climbs and bends left, then right, then left, and may be blocked beyond that point. There is no signpost or marker, but the idea is to leave the track by turning right, then find a way straight up a rugged, wooded slope. There is a winding path, but it is very overgrown and needs clearing. However, there are cairns up a slope of moss-covered boulders and a gap in a fence at the top. Join a grassy track in low

woodland and turn right, passing a signpost at a water trough at **Caraju e Creccos**, at 275m (900ft).

Walk along and up the grassy track, passing a stone hut and continuing up a gravel track past lentisc bushes. Follow the track gently downhill, bending left and uphill past **Funtana Su Mudregu**, at 280m (920ft). The track climbs a bushy slope to reach a fine pinnettu thatched with brushwood and a picnic site at **Su Mudregu**, at 330m (1080ft). There are fine views across the reservoir of Lago Omodeo, with mountains rising higher.

Turn right through a gateway, following a track flanked by drystone walls past fields. Rise uphill, with a farm to the left, and continue straight ahead up to a road and track junction beside a concrete hut at **Sa Serra**, at 342m (1120ft). Follow the track, which is flanked by drystone walls, rising gently past fields where the biggest trees are cork oaks. A gentle descent leads to a signpost, where a wooden hut and a mapboard stand well to the left at **Preda e Cuba**, at 340m (1115ft). ◀

It is worth turning right here and walking down a track to find a domus de janas on the right.

Follow the main track ahead, as signposted for 'Ponte Fiume Taloro', undulating, but generally descending. The track is gravel as it passes masses of asphodel, running through cork oak woods and heading down a slope of lentisc bushes. Pass a hut and let a clearer track lead past cork oak trees to a road and gates. Turn right down the road, reaching a junction before a bridge, **Ponte Fiume Taloro**, at 130m (425ft).

WALK 50
Sedilo and Nuraghe Iloi

Distance	8km (5 miles)
Start/finish	Centre of Sedilo
Total ascent/descent	75m (245ft)
Time	2hrs 30min
Map	IGMI 'Serie 50' 515, 'Serie 25' 515 I
Terrain	Easy walking along roads, tracks and short, rugged paths
Refreshment	Bars in Sedilo
Transport/access	Regular daily buses serve Sedilo from Cagliari, Abbasanta and Nuoro
Note	Route uses waymarked trail 610

This short and easy walk is very handy for anyone travelling along the main road between Cagliari and Nuoro. The route links the well-preserved archaeological sites of Nuraghe Iloi and the Necropoli di Ispiluncas, which both lie outside the little town of Sedilo.

Start in the centre of **Sedilo** and follow a straight road, Via Carlo Alberto, towards the edge of town. The last big building along this road is a school in a green space.

Nuraghe Iloi stands high above several hut circles in the countryside near Sedilo

191

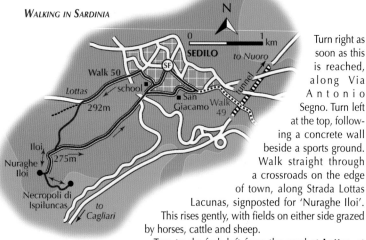

Turn right as soon as this is reached, along Via Antonio Segno. Turn left at the top, following a concrete wall beside a sports ground. Walk straight through a crossroads on the edge of town, along Strada Lottas Lacunas, signposted for 'Nuraghe Iloi'. This rises gently, with fields on either side grazed by horses, cattle and sheep.

Two tracks fork left from the road at **Lottas**, at 292m (958ft), so follow the one furthest left. The track is clear, flanked by fields, lentisc bushes and drystone walls. When the track ends, walk straight ahead along a rugged path, bouldery underfoot, flanked by drystone walls and scrub. Avoid all turnings and note that the path is accompanied by tall concrete posts carrying a power line. Join a tarmac road at a signpost and turn right. The road becomes a track at **Iloi**, at 275m (900ft), ending with a parking space for a Parco Archeologico. A path leads straight towards the well-preserved stone tower of **Nuraghe Iloi**, which is surrounded by the inter-linked foundations of hut circles.

Backtrack to the parking space and follow a broad, stone-paved path. This narrows as it drops steep and rugged, levelling out on a slope of olives. Head down again, watching for red/white markers, as the path is vague, and levelling out at a big notice for the **Necropoli di Ispiluncas**. A series of square-cut entrances lead into elaborate rock tombs. Climb back up the path to return to **Iloi**.

Walk along the track and tarmac road, heading directly for Sedilo, passing fields grazed by horses, cattle and sheep, often overwhelmed by lentisc and other scrub. The road runs up and down, reaching a well-signposted crossroads on the edge of Sedilo. It is possible to walk straight ahead, past the school, and back into the centre along Via Carlo Alberto. Alternatively, to extend the walk a little, turn right at the school as signposted for 'San Constantino' and the 'Museo del Territorio'. Use a stone-paved path beside the road, and as the road bends left, pass the chapel of **San Gaicomo**, at 270m (885ft). There are views of a racecourse and the reservoir of Lago Omodeo, with mountains beyond. Around the next bend, a paved path leads to a viewpoint. At the end of Viale San Giacomo, it is possible to turn right and launch straight into Walk 49, or to turn left and follow Corso Eleonora back into the centre of **Sedilo**.

The Necropoli di Ispiluncas features a hillside carved with several domus de janas

APPENDIX A

Route summary table

No	Title	Distance	Time	Terrain	Page
1	Monte Ortobene from Nuoro	16km (10 miles)	5hrs	Roads and tracks, from farmland to wooded slopes, and a steep wooded path for the descent	35
2	Monte Corrasi from Oliena	12 or 20km (7½ or 12½ miles)	4 or 6hrs	A road and track climb high into the mountains, with rugged paths over the highest parts	38
3	Punta Ortu Camminu and Sos Nidos	21km (13 miles)	7hrs	A road and track climb high into the mountains, with very rough and rocky ground on the highest parts. A steep and stony descent into woods.	43
4	Punta Cusidore from Nostra Signora di Monserrata	13km (8 miles)	5hrs	Easy roads and tracks on cultivated and wooded slopes give way to steep scree and steeper rock, requiring hands-on scrambling	46
5	Tiscali from Valle di Lanaittu	7km (4½ miles)	3hrs	Easy woodland tracks, then steep and rocky paths, with some scrambling	49
6	Tiscali via Scala de Surtana	10km (6 miles)	4hrs	Two stretches of steep, rocky paths that require scrambling, separated by an easy woodland path	52
7	Gola de Su Gorropu	8 or 13km (5 or 8 miles)	3hrs 30min	Good tracks and paths down a steep slope. Gentle paths and tracks through a well-wooded valley.	55
8	Dorgali, Monte Bardia and Cala Gonone	11km (6½ miles)	4hrs	Easy paths become very rocky and stony, requiring careful route-finding in woodland, with some mild scrambling	58
9	Dorgali and Cala Gonone	16km (10 miles)	5hrs	Woodland tracks and paths, with some road-walking	61

No	Title	Distance	Time	Terrain	Page
10	Genna 'e Petta and Sa Portiscra	8km (5 miles)	3hrs	A track gives way to a rough and stony path on rocky, wooded slopes	65
11	Codula Luna and Cala Gonone	25km (15½ miles)	8hrs	A track and rugged paths descend into the valley. A riverside path gives way to a rugged riverbed. A popular coast path and road are used at the end.	67
12	Cala Sisine, Cala Luna and Cala Gonone	25km (15½ miles)	8hrs	Good valley track at first, then rough and stony paths uphill and downhill, sometimes near the coast, ending with a road-walk	70
13	Giustizieri and Sa Coronas	13 or 19km (8 or 12 miles)	3hrs 30min or 5hrs	Gentle and obvious tracks rise and fall on slopes of macchia	75
14	Genna Silana to Genna Croce	11km (7 miles)	6hrs	Rocky and pathless, needing care throughout, with some scrambling	78
15	Coile Orbisi and Sa Pischina	15km (9½ miles)	5hrs	Good woodland tracks at the start and finish, with rugged paths and rocky slopes in the middle	81
16	Fennau, Televai and Urzulei	9 or 17km (5½ or 10½ miles)	2hrs 30min or 5hrs	Easy roads and tracks at first, but rugged paths and a steep, wooded descent at the end	84
17	Talana and Nuraghe Bau e Tanca	11km (7 miles)	4hrs	Roads, forest tracks and a few rugged paths	88
18	Monte Olinie to Coe Serra	13km (8 miles)	4hrs	Mostly downhill on good tracks and paths, on slopes of scrub and forest	91

No	Title	Distance	Time	Terrain	Page
19	Talana and Coe Serra	16km (10 miles)	6hrs	Paths through macchia, tracks through forest, rugged riverbeds and road	95
20	Sa Mola and Paule Munduge	10 or 15km (6 or 9½ miles)	3hrs 30min or 5hrs	Easy tracks and rugged paths, steep at times, on wooded and rocky slopes	98
21	Santa Maria Navarrese and Monte Oro	15 or 17km (9½ or 10½ miles)	4 or 5hrs	Narrow, stony paths across rocky, scrub woodland slopes, with an optional climb to a rocky peak	101
22	Baunei and Punta Giradili	16km (10 miles)	7hrs	Extensive areas of macchia and steep, rocky slopes. Roads and tracks are used for much of the way, with steep and rugged linking paths.	104
23	Irbidossili and Cala Goloritzè	17km (10½ miles)	5hrs	Good tracks at the start and finish, with steep and rugged paths in between, often on well-wooded slopes	109
24	Golgo and Cala Goloritzè	9km (5½ miles)	3hrs	Well-wooded, rugged limestone with a clear, obvious, rough and stony path	112
25	Serra Ovara and Cala Sisine	18 or 20.5km (11 or 12½ miles)	7hrs	A narrow path up a broad, rocky, wooded crest. An awkward descent requires careful route-finding. An easy valley track to finish.	115
26	Genna Sesole to Golgo	13km (8 miles)	4hrs	Good tracks and rugged riverbeds in well-wooded valleys	119
27	Genna Ramene to Golgo	8km (5 miles)	2hrs 30min	Easy walking along a track through a well-wooded valley	122
28	Triei and Osono	16km (10 miles)	5hrs	Minor roads and forest tracks, although some short sections are very rough and stony	125

No	Title	Distance	Time	Terrain	Page
29	Perda Pera and Monte Arista	8km (5 miles)	3hrs	Steep and well-wooded paths, ending with an easy road walk	128
30	Ulassai, Canyon and Punta Matzeu	8 or 9km (5 or 5½ miles)	3hrs	Some steep, rugged, wooded paths, along with roads and tracks	130
31	Ulassai and Baulassa	15 or 19km (9½ or 12 miles)	6 or 7hrs	Rugged woodland paths, as well as easy tracks and roads	133
32	Osini and Nuraghe Serbissi	16 or 24km (10 or 15 miles)	5 or 7hrs	Mostly along roads and clear tracks through well-wooded hills	137
33	Taquisara and Is Tostoinus	12km (7½ miles)	4hrs	Rugged hill paths, forest tracks and roads	140
34	Perda Liana from Genna Filigi	3 or 10km (2 or 6¼ miles)	1hr 30min or 4hrs	Either a short, stony path from Pinningassu and back, or a longer walk on roads, tracks and paths, on open and wooded slopes, sometimes steep	143
35	Laconi and Santa Sofia	19km (12 miles)	6hrs	Well-wooded parkland paths, as well as forest tracks and roads, through gentle rolling countryside	146
36	Funtanamela and Gurduxiones	9km or 10km (5½ or 6 miles)	3hrs	Easy and gently graded forest tracks over low hills	150
37	Punta La Marmora from S'Arena	15km (9½ miles)	5hrs	Clear paths across gentle and rocky slopes onto the highest mountains	152
38	Punta La Marmora from Bruncu Spina	15km (9½ miles)	5hrs	A good track onto a mountain crest, then rugged, with some good paths and some vague paths	155
39	Punta La Marmora from Cuile Meriagus	15km (9½ miles)	5hrs	Good tracks and paths on wooded and rugged slopes	158

No	Title	Distance	Time	Terrain	Page
40	Arcu Guddetorgiu and Girgini	28km (17½ miles)	9hrs	Mostly roads and tracks with gentle gradients, but also some rugged paths across steep slopes. Lower parts are wooded, especially towards the end.	160
41	Monte Spada from Genna Luddurreo	6.5km (4 miles)	2hrs 30min	A clear track to the summit, followed by a rugged descent. Tracks and rough, wooded paths around the mountain slopes.	163
42	Tonara and Punta Muggianeddu	15 or 13.5km (9½ or 8½ miles)	5hrs	Clear roads and forest tracks, with paths used on higher slopes	166
43	Baueri, Passo Perdu Abes and Tonara	15km (9½ miles)	5hrs	Good forest and hillside tracks, climbing/falling gradually	169
44	Meana Sardo to Aritzo	31 or 32km (19¼ or 19¾ miles)	10hrs	Mostly along clear forest tracks and linking paths, as well as roads and a railway line	172
45	Aritzo and Geratzia	10km (6¼ miles)	3hrs	Rugged hillside paths, good woodland tracks and mountain roads	177
46	Teti and S'Urbale	8km (5 miles)	2hrs 30min	The ascent is by road and the descent uses clear tracks, mostly on wooded slopes	179
47	Teti and Craru Eridunele	12km (7½ miles)	4hrs	Minor roads, farm tracks and forest tracks, mostly on gentle slopes	182
48	Sorradile and Monte Cresia	14km (8½ miles)	4hrs	Roads, tracks and occasional paths on wooded and farmed slopes	184
49	Sedilo to Ponte Fiume Taloro	16km (10 miles)	5hrs	Mostly roads at first, then farm and forest tracks with one rugged ascent	187
50	Sedilo and Nuraghe Iloi	8km (5 miles)	2hrs 30min	Easy walking along roads, tracks and short, rugged paths	190

APPENDIX B

Glossary

Topographic features

Place-names on maps of Sardinia are written in Sard – a language quite distinct from Italian. Many place-names describe the nature of the terrain and features in the countryside, so it is useful to be able to translate some of the more common elements. For each word, the first column gives various Sard dialect forms that you might see.

Sard	English	Sard	English
arcada/arcu	arch	muflones	mouflon/wild sheep
bacu/bau	gorge or valley	nuraghe	circular stone tower
bruncu/fruncu	hill summit	oro	gold
cala	sandy beach	parco	park
camminu	path	paule	small lake
campu/campo	field/plain	perda/preda/predu	stone
chiesa	church	pinnettu	shepherd's hut
coa serra/coa 'e serra	tail-end of a ridge	pischina	pool
codula	gorge or canyon	planu/pranu	plain
coile/cuile	sheepfold	ponte	bridge
costa	broad hillside	punta	point/promontory
croce	cross	rifugio	refuge
cuccuru	hill summit	riu	river
domus de janas	fairy house	ruderi	ruin
funtana	fountain	salinas	salty place
genna/enna	gap/col	San/Sant'/Santa/Santo	Saint
grotta	cave	scala	steps/stairs
janna/jenna	gap/col	sedda	saddle
longu	long	serra	ridge
meana	middle	sorgente	spring
mola	millstone	supramonte	high plateau
monte	mountain	tomba dei giganti	giant's tomb
manna/mannu	big	valle	valley

Useful Italian phrases

Although Sard is spoken widely around Sardinia, visitors would struggle to understand it. However, Italian is also spoken, and visitors will find that a few basic Italian phrases can go a long way.

Greetings and niceties

hello	*salve*
good morning	*buon giorno*
good afternoon	*buon pomeriggio*
goodnight	*buona notte*
goodbye	*arrivederci (formal)*
	ciao (informal)
see you tomorrow	*a domani*
see you later	*a più tardi*
yes/no	*sì/no*
please	*per favore*
thank you	*grazie*
that's all right	*prego*
thank you very much	*mille grazie*
excuse me	*mi scusi*
I'm sorry	*mi dispiace*

When you are struggling

I'm English/Scottish...	*sono inglese/scozzese*
I don't understand	*non capisco*
could you repeat it, please?	
	può ripeterlo, per favore?
more slowly, please	*più lentamente, per favore*
what did you say?	*ciò che ha detto?*
what is that?	*che cos'è?*
do you speak English?	*parla inglese?*
I don't speak Italian	*non parlo italiano*

Around town

there is/are, is/are there	*c'è (singular) ci sono (plural)*
is there a bank here?	*c'è una banca qui?*
where is...?	*dov'è...?*
...the post office?	*...l'ufficio postale?*
...the toilet?	*...il gabinetto/la toilette?*
men	*uomini*
women	*donne*
open/closed	*aperto/chiuso*
today/tomorrow	*oggi/domani*
next week	*la settimana prossima*
where can I buy...?	*dove posso comprare...?*
...a newspaper/stamps	*...un giornale/ francobolli*
I'd like...	*vorrei...*
I'll have this	*prendo questo*
how much?	*quanto?*

A room for the night

do you have a room?	*avete una camera?*
double/single	*doppio/singolo*
tonight	*stasera*
for two/three nights	*per due/tre notti*
how much is the room?	*quanto costa la camera?*
with bath/without bath	*con bagno/senza bagno*

Eating and drinking

drinks	*bevande*
breakfast	*prima colazione*
lunch/dinner	*pranzo/cena*
I'd like/we'd like	*vorrei/vorremmo*
I'll have/we'll have	*prendo/prendiamo*
a black coffee	*un caffè*
two black coffees	*due caffè*
white coffee	*caffè con latte / cappuccino*
three white coffees	*tre caffè con latte/ tre capuccini*
tea with milk	*tè con latte*
tea with lemon for me	*tè al limone per me*
beer	*birra*
the house wine	*il vino della casa*
a glass of red wine	*un bicchiere di vino rosso*
white wine	*vino bianco*

a bottle of water	una bottiglia d'acqua
fizzy/still	con gas/naturale
orange juice	succo d'arancia
starters	antipasti
soup	zuppa/brood
eggs, egg dishes	uova
fish, fish dishes	pesce
sea food/shellfish	frutti di mare
meat, meat dishes	carne
vegetables	verdure
I'm vegetarian	Io sono vegetariano
cheese	formaggio
fruit	frutta
ice-cream	gelato
desserts	dessert
sandwich	sandwich/panino
anything else?	altro?
nothing, thank you	niente, grazie
the bill, please	il conto, per favore
packed lunches	pranzi al sacco
two packed lunches	due pranzi al sacco
for tomorrow	per domani

Getting around Sardinia

by car/on foot	in auto/a piedi
how do I get to Nuoro?	come faccio ad arrivare a Nuoro?
where is...?	dov'è...?
...the bus station?	...la stazione dei pullman?
...the bus stop?	...la fermata del bus?
...for Lotzoraí?	...per Lotzoraí
how much is the fare?	quanto è il biglietto?
single	andata
return	andata e ritorno

Directions for walkers

where is the footpath to...?	dove si trova il sentiero per...?

may we go this way?	possiamo andare di qua?
is it far?	è lontano?
how far?	quanto è lontano?
how long?	quanto tempo ci vuole?
very near?	molto vicino?
left/right	sinistra/destra
straight on	dritto
first left	la prima a sinistra
second right	la seconda a destra
in front of the church	davanti alla chiesa
behind the hotel	dietro l'hotel
at the end of the street	alla fine della strada
after the bridge	dopo il ponte
where are you going?	dove stai andando?
I'm going/we're going to...	vado a/stiamo andando...
right of way	diritto di passaggio
no hunting	divieto di caccia
please close	si prega di chiudere
beware of the dog	attenti al cane

Days of the week

Monday	lunedi
Tuesday	martedi
Wednesday	mercoledi
Thursday	giovedi
Friday	venerdi
Saturday	sabato
Sunday	domenica

Emergencies

help! fire!	aiuto! incendio!
police	carabinieri
there's been an accident	c'è stato un incidente
call a doctor quickly	chiamate subito un medico
it's urgent!	è urgente!

APPENDIX C
Useful contacts

Travel and transport

Flights
Few direct flights operate between Britain and Sardinia, especially in the winter months. Most flights serve Cagliari, in the south of the island, and Olbia, in the north. Rather fewer serve Alghero, and this airport is the most remote from the routes in this guidebook. Airlines include Easyjet www.easyjet.com, Ryanair www.ryanair.com, Jet2 www.jet2.com, BMI Baby www.bmidbaby.com, and British Airways www.ba.com. If the little airport at Arbatax was developed in the future, this would offer immediate access to the bulk of the walks covered in this guide. At the time of writing, it is served from Rome by Meridiana www.meridiana.it.

Ferries
Ferryports at Cagliari and Olbia link with Italian ports, and most ferries are operated by Moby Lines www.moby.it and Tirrenia www.tirrenia.it. An occasional ferry from Civitavecchia to Arbatax, leading directly to the area covered by this guidebook, is operated by Tirrenia. There are other ports and operators, and sailings from France and Spain, but these are less useful as they berth further from the area covered by the guide.

Buses and timetables
Azienda Regionale Sarda Trasporti (ARST) www.arst.sardegna.it
Information is available only in Italian, and English-speakers will struggle to use the site, but all the detail about routes and timetables is there. Such detailed information is not available in Sardinia, so print out the ones you need!

Separate bus companies operate in and around the main towns, including CTM in Cagliari, ASPO in Olbia, and ATP in Nuoro.

Tourist Information
Whole of Sardinia www.sardegnaturismo.it
Province of Nuoro www.provincia.nuoro.it
Province of Ogliastra www.turismo.ogliastra.it
Accommodation options can be checked on the provincial websites. For Ogliastra, use the 'Turismo' link, followed by 'Guida all'Ospitalità'. For Ogliastra, use the 'Dove Dormire' link.

Tourist information offices are available at
Nuoro, Piazza Italia, tel 0784-238878
Oliena, Piazza Berlinguer, tel 0784-286078
Dorgali, Via Lamarmora, tel 0784-96243
Cala Gonone, Viale Bue Marino, tel 0784-93696
Santa Maria Navarrese, Piazza Principessa, tel 0782-614037
Tortolì, Via Mazzini, tel 0782-622824
Meana Sardo, Via Montebello, tel 0784-64179
Aritzo, Via Umberto, tel 0784-627235
Desulo, Via Lamarmora, tel 338-2501654
Fonni, Via Zunnui, tel 0784-57197

Maps
Michelin and DeAgostini publish road maps of Sardinia at 1:200,000. Government maps are published by the Instituto Geografico Militare d'Italia (IGMI) at 1:25,000 and 1:50,000. Coverage can be checked online at www.igmi.org/ware.

Maps can be ordered direct from IGMI, or from The Map Shop, 15 High Street, Upton-upon-Severn, WR8 0HJ, tel 01684 593146, www.themapshop.co.uk.

An excellent series of maps covering waymarked trails is published free of charge by the Sardinian forestry agency, Ente Foreste delle Sardegna, www.sardegnaambiente.it/foreste, at a scale of 1:25,000. These can be studied online and printed, by clicking first on the 'Sentieri' link, then click on each area, then click the 'Scarica la carta' link to find the maps.

The Lemon House
The Lemon House is a guest house at Lotzoraì, run by Peter Herold and Anne McGlone. They offer particular assistance to outdoor enthusiasts, covering such diverse activities as walking, rock-climbing, cycling, kayaking and general touring. They can help, if necessary, with guiding and accompanying their guests, and with language issues. Useful for cautious, first-time visitors.

The Lemon House
Via Dante 19
08040 Lotzoraì (OG)
Italy
Tel 0782 669 507
www.peteranne.it

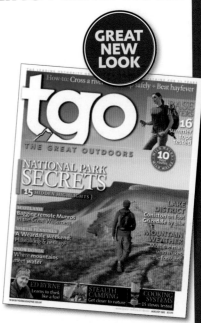

LISTING OF CICERONE GUIDES

For full information on all our guides, and to order books and eBooks, visit our website: **www.cicerone.co.uk**.

Walking – Trekking – Mountaineering – Climbing – Cycling

Over 40 years, Cicerone have built up an outstanding collection of 300 guides, inspiring all sorts of amazing adventures.

Every guide comes from extensive exploration and research by our expert authors, all with a passion for their subjects. They are frequently praised, endorsed and used by clubs, instructors and outdoor organisations.

All our titles can now be bought as **e-books** and many as iPad and Kindle files and we will continue to make all our guides available for these and many other devices.

Our website shows any **new information** we've received since a book was published. Please do let us know if you find anything has changed, so that we can pass on the latest details. On our **website** you'll also find some great ideas and lots of information, including sample chapters, contents lists, reviews, articles and a photo gallery.

It's easy to keep in touch with what's going on at Cicerone, by getting our monthly **free e-newsletter**, which is full of offers, competitions, up-to-date information and topical articles. You can subscribe on our home page and also follow us on **Facebook** and **Twitter**, as well as our **blog**.

Cicerone – the very best guides for exploring the world.

CICERONE

2 Police Square Milnthorpe Cumbria LA7 7PY
Tel: 015395 62069 info@cicerone.co.uk
www.cicerone.co.uk